FULL BODY SCAM

The Naked View of Current Airport Security

David H. Brown

authorHOUSE®

AuthorHouse™
1663 Liberty Drive
Bloomington, IN 47403
www.authorhouse.com
Phone: 1-800-839-8640

First published by AuthorHouse 7/11/2011

ISBN: 978-1-4634-2960-7 (sc)
ISBN: 978-1-4634-3047-4 (e)

OTHER BOOKS BY DAVID H. BROWN

I Would Rather Be Audited By The IRS Than Give A Speech (1995)

NINE/ELEVEN (2004)

Airline Passenger Screening Has Become a FEMA-TYPE SNAFU (2006)

Operation Red Herring (2007)

The Decoration/Memorial Day War (2008)

Murder at 250 Center Street (2009)

Life Is Just A Bowl Of Memories (2010)

Next In Line To The Oval Office (2011)

CONTENTS

FULL BODY SCAM

The Naked View Of Current Airport Security

FOREWORD

This book reflects the 10th anniversary of the infamous terrorist skyjacking of three U.S. aircraft on September 11, 2001.

It is not an ordinary one because it will be in three sections. The first, which is the new title, is an update on airport security procedures. The second and third are previous books I have written on this subject – NINE/ELEVEN, and AIRLINE PASSENGER SCREENING HAS BECOME A FEMA-TYPE SNAFU.

My unique perspective comes from having been the press officer for the Federal Aviation Administration's Task Force on the Deterrence of Air Piracy. I am the last surviving member of the original 9-member team. The group was formed in 1969 following a mandate by Congress to deal with the recurring skyjacking of aircraft, mainly to Cuba.

The previous books depict the work of our Task Force and how it developed the original passenger screening procedure. Three of us traveled to nine airports during 1969-70 to test the Dailey Profile as Step One in the system. The results, revealed in the two other books, should have been the basis for current procedures. But, well before 9/11 – in fact, some 30 years before that – the Profile as Step One was brushed aside in favor of subjecting every passenger – young and old – to be electronically screened first.

Those previous books indicate why I challenge the basis for such a change, which not only continues to this day but has been "enhanced." My premise is that this is a waste of time and money because the original approach would accomplish the same intended ends without humiliating passengers and often unnecessarily delaying their flights. Bureaucratic intransigence must give way to "outside-the-box" flexibility.

Many thanks go to my son, Mark, and to my oldest professional friend, Wes Pedersen, for their invaluable help and encouragement.

David H. Brown(airportscreening@aol.com)

CHAPTER ONE —
ARE YOU KIDDING ME?

In January 2009, a Transportation Security Administration officer conducted a body search of a 3 year-old girl. In April 2011, another similar incident occurred at a different airport, this time involving a 6 year-old girl. Both of those children were searched at "random." In May 2011, an 8 month-old child was subjected to a pat down because her stroller set off an alarm.

The excuse given for such intrusions is that Middle East terrorists often use children for some of their deadly efforts. But, this is not the Middle East.

Each administration since 9/11 has adopted the assumption that all domestic airline passengers are potential Middle East terrorists. That not only includes the likes of 3 and 6 year-old children, but "mature" individuals in their 80s and 90s. But, to the TSA, its credo is a convoluted interpretation of President Franklin D. Roosevelt's admonition during World War II that "the only thing we have to fear is fear itself."

The TSA fears everyone. Strangely, the Constitution states in the Fourth Amendment that a person is presumed innocent when it comes to search. There has to be a "reasonable" indication that a person has to be searched. There was no such assumption in the cases of the two tots.

Random search has yet to prove it has deterred any Middle East skyjacking attempt. It should be called the "needle in the haystack" search. The government abrogated the Fourth Amendment in the name of "war." But, what is the definition of that term? According to the dictionary, "war" constitutes **armed conflict**. Our government declared the end of combat in Iraq. That is not the case in Afghanistan. If combat has ended in Iraq, then one would assume the protection under the Fourth Amendment should be reinstated.

As far as research goes, the United States never declared war in those two Middle East countries because the "enemy" was not the organized governments there. In Iraq, it is Al Qaeda; in Afghanistan, it is the Taliban.

If police departments in the U.S. could abrogate the Fourth Amendment, then they could conduct their own random searches without "probable cause."

CHAPTER TWO —
CATCH ME IF YOU CAN

The TSA seems to have a search procedure de jour. The notorious "No Fly" list seems to have resulted more in embarrassment than in accomplishment. What Middle East terrorist in his or her right mind would use a name that was known to law enforcement authorities? What Middle East terrorist in his or her right mind would wear clothing that would call attention to them? The 19 Middle East terrorists looked and acted like any other passenger.

In an online article posted on November 20, 2010, independent airline industry consultant Robert Herbst wrote: "It's absurd to focus on 100% of our screening resources on 100% of the passengers when real life screening should focus on the 5-10% who behave suspiciously."

He had the right idea, slightly wrong data, and a misconception. As my previous books have noted, the Task Force concluded that it field tests concluded only 5-10ths of 1% of the flying public needed special screening, using as Step One the nearly two dozen elements of the Dailey Profile. (A "suspect" only needed to tick off any half dozen of those elements.) And, acting "suspiciously" was not deemed a major reason to be alerted.

The success of the Dailey Profile was part "psychological warfare." Potential skyjackers – domestic or international – never knew all of the elements. The press has reported on some of them from time to time, but never the entire list. That alone was a deterrent. Current screening procedures are widely known, so a potential skyjacker only needs to observe to avoid suspicion.

What the TSA has caught have been domestic skyjackers, albeit some with ties to Middle East terrorists. What the TSA has kept from getting on flights are domestic weapons, not "improvised explosive devices" (IEDs) used by Middle East terrorists.

The 19 Middle East terrorists were successful (although one plane crashed in Pennsylvania) for two reasons – intelligence dysfunction, and the ability to gain access to the cockpits. Of the latter, simply keeping the cockpit doors double-locked during flight has been a major deterrent. (This had been recommended by Task Force member Lowell Davis.)

The Task Force determined to have the trust of airlines and their passengers. The team took the view of "to catch a thief you have to think like a thief." Members tried to think like a potential skyjacker.

Government security officials, in their zeal to deal with a perceived recurrence of 9/11, have adopted screening procedures aimed at Middle East terrorists but applying them to innocent domestic passengers. A later chapter will explore this in detail.

CHAPTER THREE —
TRUST ME, I'M FROM THE GOVERNMENT

Most airline passengers today accept whatever the government determines is in their safety. The TSA, now part of the Department of Homeland Security, has this statement on its website: "Federal courts (have) upheld warrantless searches of carry-on luggage. Courts characterize the routine administration search (of passengers) conducted at a security checkpoint as a warrantless search, *subject to the reasonableness requirements of the Fourth Amendment. Such a warrantless search, also known as an administrative search, is valid under the Fourth Amendment if it is 'no more intrusive or intensive than necessary, in light of current technology, to detect weapons or explosives,' confined in good faith to that purpose."* (Emphasis mine.)

The key to conducting warrantless searches lies in TSA's own words – "reasonableness requirements of the Fourth Amendment." Also, note that this refers only to "searches of carry-on luggage." How do such warrantless searches apply to electronic scanning and pat downs of passengers without reason to suspect such people are potential Middle East skyjackers?

When the Task Force tested the Dailey Profile, it had the Fourth Amendment (on search and seizure) foremost in mind. The elements of the Profile resulted from *facts*, not assumptions. The Profile not only was endorsed by the American Civil Liberties Union, but also was ruled constitutional in a New York Federal Court case.

Major airlines at first did not trust the work of the Task Force. After all, the research was confined to one airline, Eastern, which had been the most skyjacked at the time. However, when the Profile was applied to *all* airlines at New Orleans with the same results, it was accepted as Step One.

During the testing phase, press conferences were held at each of the 9 airports. The media did not know that I videotaped reaction from passengers when they were told they were being "screened" for security purposes. *Not one passenger refused to board, knowing this. In fact, some said they only would fly an airline with such protection.* As a result, the Task Force not only gained the trust of the airlines, but also of the passengers. That trust is in question today.

The government continues to make the argument that current measures are needed to prevent another 9/11. This book argues the same end can be obtained with a minimum of intrusion at the gate by adapting the Dailey Profile to the current situation and returning it to Step One in the passenger screening process.

＊ ＊ ＊ ＊ ＊

From available information, all 19 of the 9/11 Middle East terrorists fit the required six elements of the Dailey Profile. However, the Profile no longer had been Step One in the screening process.

A clear understanding of the Task Force's work is detailed in its Final Report issued in *1978*! It remains a public document that can be purchased from the National Technical Information Service in paper or electronic form. Document number is #ADA076457. By the way, Page 93 predicted what turned out to be 9/11!

When officials of the DHS or TSA are asked how many Middle East terrorist skyjacking attempts have been thwarted, the answer is, "That is classified information." The Task Force dealings with the news media once were described as one of the most successful government programs. Our motto was this: "You cannot eliminate all crime, so you cannot eliminate all attempts at skyjacking. Our aim is to reduce the odds to a manageable number." That is why the term "Deterrence" was the official designation of intent. We dealt in reality, not fear. With the focus on that 5-10ths of 1% of the flying public, the Task Force believed security would be more effective than trying to screen 100% of the flying public.

CHAPTER FOUR

WHY NOT DO WHAT THE ISRAELIS DO?

One of the first things the Task Force did in 1969 was to consider the procedures used by El Al Airlines. It concluded what worked in Israel would not work in the U.S. Israel has been on war footing since the 1948 creation of that nation. It is surrounded by "enemies." It could use measures not readily acceptable in this country. Also, Israel only has a miniscule fraction of the more than 30,000 daily domestic flights throughout the U.S.

In November 2010, the former chief of security for El Al – Isaac Yeffet – told a reporter for a leading independent news site Newmax.com: "Every (El Al) passenger has to be interviewed by a well-trained agent before check-in. Agents then perform electronic body scans or searches only on those who arouse suspicions during the interview."

Does that not remind one of using the Dailey Profile as Step One?

Yeffet was highly critical of U.S. procedures. "The U.S. Transportation Safety Administration (sic) 'wants to tell me we now have security in (the U.S.). This is an illusion. Technology in general can never replace a qualified and well-trained human being. (This will be discussed in the next chapter.) It is unnecessary to search 'innocent people.'" He went on to explain that "security should instead focus on determining if a passenger is suspicious by intensely interviewing them. We at El Al have used the hand/body search for so many years, but we did it only to suspicious passengers." He also said that the El Al procedure has enabled the airline to "identify the right people."

There is no argument that electronic search is necessary. But, there are two aspects. All baggage should be searched that way. But, as Yeffet pointed out, not all passengers should be searched that way. The sight of children, as well as elderly people in wheelchairs, being either searched electronically and by pat down is not what the Israelis do.

CHAPTER FIVE

ELECTRONIC SCANNING AND PAT DOWNS EFFECTIVE?

TSA scanners are not medically-trained radiologists. They are government employees (who now are being courted by unions). Each one has to "read" perhaps hundreds of images each shift in rapid succession. How accurate can they be?

When you have medical electronic scanning, it is done carefully and individually. Afterwards, it is analyzed by a trained medical person. The airport scanning process is like a mass production line in a factory. Where is the quality control? There are continuing reports of scanners missing vital "evidence" that would – and/or should – alert security personnel for further investigation. TSA and even the airlines themselves run tests, and the results sometimes are embarrassing.

If electronic scanning makes many passengers uncomfortable, pat downs are worse. We trust medically-trained professions to make such examinations, but TSA personnel are not in that category. Yet, passengers young and old, healthy and infirm, are subjected to such personal intrusions.

Why do government officials continue to use these two procedures as Step One, especially in "random inspection" situations? It is in the unrealistic assumption this priority will prevent a recurrence of 9/11. That might justify the procedure for flights that originate outside of the U.S. But, we cannot control security measures in foreign countries. And, sometimes, that creates a disaster.

In December 2005, a flight from South America landed at Miami International Airport. As the passengers were about to deplane, a man charged through the crowd and demanded to get off. According to news reports, someone shouted, "He has a bomb!" Two of the passengers were armed U.S. marshals – one male, one female. They chased after the man as he got to the jet way and ordered him to stop. They later reported he seemed to be reaching into his pocket, so they fired. A total of 11 bullets struck the man, killing him.

According to news reports, the victim's wife was shouting that he forgot to take his medication. But, her Spanish accent may not have been heard correctly. An investigation took six months to complete, and concluded that the marshals' action was justified even though no weapon was found on the victim. They each received a commendation.

Can we assume the victim passed security inspection prior to departure? Can't we wonder why a perceived terrorist would wait until a plane had landed before he would take action, especially with his wife aboard?

＊ ＊ ＊ ＊ ＊

On May 10, 2011, AolNews.Huffpost reported that a passenger on an American Airlines flight to San Francisco from Chicago rushed to the cockpit door and pounded on it just as the aircraft approached the airport. Several passengers – including a flight attendant, a retired Secret Service agent and a retired San Mateo, CA police officer – subdued him. RagehAlmurisi, a 28 year-old resident of Vallejo, CA, had a Yemeni passport. The obvious question is: How did Almurisi pass security at O'Hare International Airport?

There have been other such incidents, according to that report. On a Continental Airlines flight from Houston to Chicago, a 34 year-old man tried to open one of the plane's doors. He was questioned, but later released. Another report involved the forced deplaning of two passengers in Middle East attire because other passengers felt "uncomfortable" with them on board.

CHAPTER SIX —
MIDDLE EAST TERRORISTS VS. DOMESTIC FANATICS

There is an ocean of different between the two entities listed in this title. Perhaps the problem with current airport security is that the government does not believe there is a difference.

My two earlier books dealt with domestic fanatics by and large. I also identified the flash point that changed the priorities the Task Force established, tested, and verified as when Arab terrorists skyjacked four U.S. aircraft in the early fall of 1970. Despite the fact that these events took place in the Middle East, but not on American soil, the Nixon administration ordered the FAA to forget about the Dailey Profile as Step One and instead electronically screen every passenger. To get around the protection of the Fourth Amendment, the rationale was that acts of terrorism mirrored war. This then resulted in every passenger to be presumed a Middle East terrorist. As a result, every passenger was presumed to be "guilty" and had to prove his or her innocence by being subjected to electronic screening. In a previous chapter, I pointed out this disregarded the vital word of "reasonableness."

If the government wanted tangible results of security without intrusive "search," it simply could establish two procedures – one for Middle East terrorists, and another for domestic fanatics. Terrorists want to do bodily harm; domestic fanatics generally want to "make a statement" or to settle a grudge.

It would not take a major effort to update, develop, and test separate Profile procedures. They must be based on unbiased statistics, as was the Dailey Profile. Government officials could get proper guidance from reading the Task Force Final Report, and adapt that approach to current conditions nationally and internationally.

CHAPTER SEVEN —
1+1 DOES NOT EQUAL 3

Mathematics dictates that if a basic assumption/premise is wrong, whatever follows is wrong. If the assumption/premise that Middle East terrorism is the same as domestic fanaticism is wrong, therefore what develops from this also is wrong. Current security procedures have caused consternation and even distrust by the traveling public. This could be why we keep having security procedures de jour.

If electronic screening of everyone is valid, what is the explanation for the former Secretary of the DHS Tom Ridge having to be "searched?" All he had to do was produce an ID card. I had a titanium hip operation a few years ago. My doctor gave me a special medical alert card with that information. A short time later, when I was trying to board a flight, I offered to present that document to a security officer, knowing I would set off the electronic device. He replied, "Not interested." A full body search ensued. I now have a pacemaker with a similar document. The device will be compromised during an electronic full body scan. As a result, I will have to submit to a pat down procedure. No matter that I also have a valid passport with my photo ID, as well as the latest "smart" military ID card also with my photo. TSA could save a lot of time and money by examining the documents. Of course, I do not mind luggage being electronically scanned, but there have been too many stories about such searches missing weapons.

It does not help TSA's cause when situations of "abuse" are reported in the media. In November 2010, a Michigan man who survived bladder cancer had to wear a "urine bag" attached to a tube in his abdomen. At the security station, he asked to be taken to a private room for "screening." Despite his plea that a public pat down would break the seal of his bag, a security officer did just that. Urine spilled over the would-be traveler.

Then, there are humorous situations, but perhaps not funny to TSA officers. One editorial cartoon showed an elderly woman at a security checkpoint stating, "Oh, I'm not flying anywhere. I'm just here for the pat down." Another cartoon depicted a Christmas Eve scene with a child looking at Santa's empty bag. "Sorry, kid," the jolly one said, "the TSA got it all in the pat down."

On a more serious side, India's ambassador to the U.S. was trying to board a flight in December 2010 at Jackson, MS. She was dressed in her native attire, which caused the TSA screener to order a second security procedure. Her ID attesting to her high political office was ignored. The TSA explained that anyone with "bulky clothing" had to be specially "searched."

On June 18, 2011, a 95 year-old woman was stopped by security officials at a Florida airport and was subjected to a pat down. It seems her adult diaper was "wet and firm." Security officials removed the diaper. How bureaucratic can the TSA get?

On July 6, 2011, the TSA warned that "terrorists were considering implanting bombs in air travelers." TV comedians did not have to write any other material for their monologues that night.

CHAPTER EIGHT

A REALITY CHECK

The Department of Homeland Security and its Transportation Security Administration have to forget bureaucracy and deal in reality.

If those two government agencies have not done so already, its top officials should convene a conference with like counterparts in the aviation industry to develop a new "battle" plan. There should be room for skeptics and "open minds." They need to regain the trust of the flying public, while at the same time improve airport security procedures. Those procedures need to be tested in a realistic manner before being introduced. (These also must deal with security at all forms of transportation involving both the public and cargo shippers.)

There are those who will assert this approach is "unpatriotic" because it challenges the government's continued "searching" of every airline passenger as Step One. The Task Force concluded early on that whatever procedure we developed had to be effective while facilitating the boarding of passengers. The TSA's response to this is to hire more screeners. We should not be making the boarding process more difficult while assuring passengers security procedures will provide as much protection as possible. The Task Force subscribed to the adage, "An ounce of prevention is worth a pound of cure." While it focused most of its efforts on preventing a potential skyjacker from boarding a plane, it also made provisions for dealing with such an event in the air. At least one device has remained secret to this day, as far as I can discern. Airlines were briefed on this 100% fatal device, but refused to adopt it.

During the Task Force's testing phase, it told the airlines there was no way to totally prevent skyjacking attempts, the same way law enforcement officials say there is no way to eliminate all crime. That is the reality – harsh reality.

As the two inclusive books point out, we cannot under-estimate the zeal of terrorists. If they really want to skyjack a U.S. aircraft, they are willing to sacrifice their lives in doing so. But, as having also been noted, Middle East terrorists have easier U.S. targets of opportunity with a lot less risk. The difference between pre-9/11 and now is that we were not engaged in the Middle East conflict then.

Random searches should be eliminated because they are ineffective and too often result in humiliation both to the passenger and to the security people.

✳ ✳ ✳ ✳ ✳

The No Fly List should be re-evaluated. While it may have uncovered some domestic ne'er-do-wells, it never has prevented a repeat of 9/11. If the government wants to retain this effort, it should have realistic guidelines. Once someone is on that list, but is innocent, it literally takes heaven and earth to correct that error. That smacks of identity theft problems.

The Israel/El Al security model has the approach that can be adapted in the U.S. That is, establish guidelines for deeming a passenger "suspect." In essence, that would be an update of the Dailey Profile as Step One for domestic air travel. A different model is needed to deal with intended Middle East terrorism when it comes to air travel. In short, establish a two-tiered security system.

Our government can engage in the same "psychological warfare" approach the Task Force evolved. Tell the "enemy" only that new and more effective security procedures are in force, but skip the details. Our news media efforts presumed reporters would try to "beat the system," but they could not because they did not know all the details.

We read, see, and hear stories about how "weapons" escape detection at the gates. That is an internal problem. Government officials might want to keep in mind a bit of deception like some police departments employ. At times, an unoccupied cruiser is parked in plain sight on a major highway system. Drivers cannot be sure whether it is manned or not, but they slow down anyhow. During World War II, there were many instances of both the Allies and the Axis used "dummy" tanks and artillery weapons.

Reality requires boldness. Is our government ready to use that approach? Or, is our government content to continue using fear as its motivating rationale?

* * * * *

Two previous book -- NINE/ELEVEN and AIRLINE PASSENGER SCREENING HAS BECOME AFEMA-TYPE SNAFU -- follow.

"NINE/ELEVEN"

Could The Federal Aviation Administration Alone Have Deterred The Terrorist Skyjackers? You Will Find the Answer Here, But Not In the 9/11 Commission Report.

FOREWORD

Much has been written about the terrorists who crashed two hijacked aircraft into New York City's World Trade Center and the Pentagon in Northern Virginia on September 11, 2001. Most of the criticism aired in early 2004 before the National Commission on Terrorist Attacks Upon the United States has been focused on problems with intelligence gathering, lack of data sharing, and failure to analyze "clues."

The brunt of the commission's conclusions is directed at the Bill Clinton and George W. Bush administrations, the Central Intelligence Agency, the Department of Justice, and the Federal Bureau of Investigation. *Yet, the finger of blame has not been pointed at the one federal agency that might have prevented this catastrophe – the Federal Aviation Administration!*

This book will detail a series of foul-ups by the FAA that may well have allowed 19 terrorists to board four flights aimed at carrying out kamikaze-style missions.

Surely, our conclusions will rankle bureaucratic cages. However, my colleague, Dr. John T. Dailey, then the FAA's chief psychologist, and I are the only ones left who have personal recall on how a proven program developed by the agency's own Task Force on Deterrence of Air Piracy was turned upside down. Our work is documented in FAA Manual AM-78-35. You can buy a copy from the National Technical Information Service for about $40.

This book is the only behind-the-scenes look at how the Task Force was organized in 1969, disbanded in 1970, and its work virtually ignored from then on.

When the FAA created the Office of Civil Aviation Security in 1970, it literally became a "cop shop" that felt if you just search everybody, you are bound to turn up a hijacker. You have a better chance of winning the Lottery than accomplishing that goal.

The Manual contained the dots that should have been easily connected to deter the "9/11" terrorist hijackers. A copy probably reposes on some dusty FAA shelf.

Read how Dr. Dailey provided the key to a valid airport security system that we tested at nine airports. Read how his characteristics "profile" not only was blessed by the American Civil Liberties Union, but also was ruled constitutional in a Federal Court case.

Had those 19 terrorists been denied boarding, there still would be the twin towers at the World Trade Center. There would not have been an attack on the Pentagon. There would not have been the loss of thousands of lives. There would not be a Department of Homeland Security. There would not have been millions and millions of dollars spent on humiliating passenger searches. *And, there would not have been Afghanistan and Iraq!*

We dedicate this book to our late colleagues: Dr. H.L. (Rick) Reighard, federal air surgeon, who chaired the Task Force; Lowell L. Davis, Flight Standards Service; Max F. Collins, Aircraft Development Service; Joseph K. Blank, Office of Compliance and Security; John E. Marsh, Office of the General Counsel; E. Lee Jett, Office of International Aviation Affairs; and, Robert K. Friedman, Office of Management.

David H. Brown, Task Force press officer

WHY THIS BOOK NOW?

Dr. Dailey and I patiently tried to contact high officials in both the Executive and Legislative Branches of government, as well as the news media, with the exclusive information we had about the 1969-70 program. No one listened. Finally, we concluded that the 9-11 Commission would not consider any FAA involvement (see Appendix). A Washington Post story of 4/17/04 noted that the Commission felt the 9/11/01 hijackers might have postponed their missions if the government had announced the arrest of suspected terrorist Zacarias Moussaoui the previous month, or had publicized fears that intended to hijack jetliners.

Going public through this book was the only recourse for us to try to attract attention to what we felt was a vital aspect of 9/11/01.

We cannot comprehend why the FAA was overlooked when that agency pioneered anti-hijacking procedures involving aircraft back in 1969 when it created the Task Force.

If anyone has read the Manual in recent years, did they understand its relevance to current terrorism? All they had to do was turn to the following pages:

(39) "...there are too many people in too many parts of the world with motivations for violence to argue against expectations that (airplane hijackings) would not only spread *but become differentiated in character." (emphasis mine)*

(88) "...as times, people, motivations, and methods of operation

change, a continuing research…would be needed to meet challenges *already on the horizon." (emphasis mine)*

(93) "The Task Force was aware that *mass hijacking of U.S. aircraft could also be carried out by an organized group in order to achieve terrorist objectives." (emphasis mine)*

We respectfully submit that you do not have to be a CIA or FBI analyst to adapt these prophesies to the terrorist activity in the 1990's.

Here are five crucial decisions that we respectfully submit changed the course of history, resulted in the expenditures of millions and millions of dollars, created the Department of Homeland Security, and has inconvenienced most of the flying public:

First, in 1971, a year after the Task Force was disbanded, the FAA created an Office of Civil Aviation Security. Instead of using Task Force members as the cadre, to continue the group's work, it staffed the new organization with civil servants. It took on one Task Force member, Joe Blank, and used Lowell Davis as a "consultant."

Second, the FAA altered the sequence of the system the Task Force not only developed, but also validated. Instead of first applying a series of characteristics Dr. Dailey had developed into a "profile," it reverted to first screening by a metal detector.

Third, in 1972, the FAA ordered that *all* passengers be screened, which the Task Force found unnecessary. There is more detail on this vital aspect later in the book.

Fourth, despite increasingly violent terrorist activity almost a decade before 9/11/01, the FAA merely issued a "tepid" alert because it declared it did not have enough *hard evidence* to put airlines and airports on *high alert*.

Fifth, the Transportation Security Administration stepped into the picture after 9/11/01 and ordered *random searches*. We respectfully submit that using this procedure in hopes of catching a potential terrorist hijacker is like believing everyone has a chance to win the Lottery. However, the agency sent me a letter on January 8, 2002 arguing that random search "prevents potential terrorists from 'beating the system' by learning how it operates." Did random searches deter any of the 19 terrorists?

Later on, we will describe how the terrorists might have been deterred even using our more than 30 year-old procedure. The basic problem with all of this stems from the inability or unwillingness of bureaucrats to think like terrorists, and to examine *all possible scenarios*.

This book cannot correct the past. But, the 9-11 Commission is looking at the past to prevent the same mistakes from happening in the future. This, then, should be entered as part of the historical record. Dr. Dailey and I still anguish over 9/11/01, sincerely believing that it might have been prevented by our former agency.

On December 7, 1941, Japan attacked Pearl Harbor and nearly wiped out America's Pacific Fleet with the loss of thousands of lives. President Franklin D. Roosevelt described that event as "a date that will live in infamy." In asking Congress to declare war on that Far East enemy, his words galvanized America into a well-coordinated and well-focused retaliation.

On September 11, 2001, 19 terrorists organized by Al Qaeda in Afghanistan hijacked four aircraft; two crashed into the World Trade Center, and a third slammed into the Pentagon, causing the loss of thousands of lives. The fourth hijacked flight crashed into a Pennsylvania hillside near Stony Creek, thanks to passenger heroics. President George W. Bush did not describe 9/11/01 as "a date that will live in infamy."

He did not ask Congress to declare war on a Middle East enemy, nor did his words galvanize America into a well-coordinated and well-focused retaliation. Instead, the country's focus was turned to Iraq, which did not have any connection with 9/11/01.

The difference between these two historic events, more then 5,000 miles and 60 years apart, is that the 1940's strategy was clear-cut, while the current strategy has to be sorted out by the 9-11 Commission. The latter effort did not look into what role the FAA played, could have played, or did not play.

Most of the book is from personal recall, aided by the Manual, "The Sky Pirates" by James A. Arey, and Dr. Daily's "The Pioneer Heritage."

WHAT IF...?

In April 1975, my colleague Dr. Evan W. Pickrel and I gave a presentation to the Aerospace Medical Association in Washington DC titled, "Federal Aviation Administration's Behavioral Research Program for Defense Against Hijackings," a precursor to FAA Manual AM-78-35.

We concluded that this research appeared to be effective in checking the aerial hijacking epidemic at that time. However, it also clearly indicated that this research should continue to update results as the nature of air piracy could be expected to change.

Dr. Pickrel and I also concluded that there was a need to take advantage of new developments in computer and personal recognition technology. Before and after our retirements from the FAA, we tried repeatedly to obtain support for continued aircraft hijacking research, but to no avail.

If such research support had been given, what might the results have been? The first step would have been a scientific approach called *taxonomy* that would have provided detailed information of the *changing* types of passengers and flights. This would have aided in determining *unusual* patterns of passengers. For example, it could have noted passengers with *highly familiar traits as occurred on the four hijacked flights of 9/11/01.*

We would have had a system in place that was *maximally passenger friendly,* tried and true, with many years of experience.

It also would have been closely integrated with the anti-terrorist organizations throughout the world, as well as governmental and civil authorities with interest in the sensitivity and legality of screening systems.

The most effective value of a proper passenger screening system is the extent to which it *deters* aircraft hijacking attempts. It is highly probable that terrorist groups would not try to penetrate such an effective screening systems.

But, what about other means terrorists might use for airplanes to be lethal weapons? That is more difficult problem but an effective screening system would help counter such threats.

The behavioral profile I developed for hijackers was an application of the methodology of using items of a biographical nature to predict various types of human behavior. It was first used to predict success in pilot training. Later, it was applied to predict success in other aircrew and aviation support specialties. This same approach has been used even to predict reenlistment in the armed forces.

We did develop a screening system with minimal constitutional or civil liberties problems, a system that also was effective, less intrusive, and more economical.

John T. Dailey, Ph.D

THE PAST IS PROLOGUE

According to Dr. Dailey and his FAA colleague, Dr. E.W. Pickrel, the origin of aircraft hijackings may have occurred when the French were establishing air service across the Spanish Sahara after World War I.

The first officially reported aircraft hijacking attempt took place on February 21, 1930. Two Peruvian rebels commandeered a Pan American Airways Ford Trimotor plane and forced it to land at the city of Arequipa. They tried to force the two American pilots to fly them to Lima so they could drop propaganda leaflets over the capital city. The pilots refused to take off and were held hostage for several days. Meanwhile, British officials interceded and the rebels surrendered. There seemed to be more concern for the mail on board the plane than for the safety of the pilots, according to reports.

The first U.S. airplane hijacking occurred on May 1, 1961 when a Puerto Rican Castro sympathizer forced a National Air Lines flight from Miami to Key West to fly to Cuba. He claimed he was bringing the plane to Fidel Castro to compensate for a Cuban aircraft hijacked to the U.S. the previous year.

The incident prompted Congress to pass the Air Piracy Act. This made it a federal crime to commit or try to commit aircraft piracy; to interfere with a cockpit crewmember or flight attendant; to carry unauthorized weapons on a plane; and/or, to give false information about those crimes. It also permitted an air carrier to refuse to fly persons or property it believed would pose a safely concern in flight. The Act further called for a minimum jail sentence of 20 years, and a maximum of life imprisonment.

Almost all of the early hijackings were for political purposes. A different kind of hijacking attempt occurred on July 16, 1948 during a flight from Macao to Hong Kong. Shortly after takeoff, a group of bandits posing as passengers burst into the cockpit and killed the pilot and co-pilot. However, both victims fell forward onto the controls, and the plane crash-dived into the South China Sea. The sole survivor was one of the robbers.

The best records available state that only 12 planes were hijacked between 1930 and 1967. During 1968, there were 22 incidents; by the following year, the frequency had skyrocketed to 2-3 hijackings per week at times.

Efforts by the international community and the airline industry were frustratingly unsuccessful, despite presence of the International Civil Aviation Organization (ICAO), created by the United Nations in 1964.

In December 1969, ICAO adopted what became known as the *Tokyo Convention* that merely provided for return of hijacked aircraft to the nation of origin. A year later, it passed the *Hague Convention* that called for the punishment or extradition of aircraft hijackers. However, the choice was left up to the signers of the pact.

In September 1970, ICAO drafted a *Montreal Convention* proposing severe penalties for attacks in flight. It also recommended a treaty under which any nation that harbored aircraft hijackers, or would not extradite or prosecute them, would face an international boycott. Both efforts failed.

THE BACKGROUND OF "PROFILING"

In 1938, Dr. Dailey made his first use of "profiling" tests (multi-level or multi-stage screening measures) in his master's thesis at North Texas State University. He later developed and used such tests in screening Air Force pilots and other military specialists.

His first full time job came in 1941 when he was hired as a civilian junior test development analyst with the Office of the Air Surgeon. A short time later, he was commissioned a 2nd lieutenant and was sent to the Psychological Research Unit at San Antonio to help develop tests for pilots and crewmen. Five years later, he exchanged his major's rank for a civilian rating as director of research for the same unit developing aptitude and psychological tests for all Air Force enlisted personnel.

Dr. Daily earned his doctorate in 1949. Two years later, he became chief scientist at the Bureau of Naval Personnel in Washington, DC, directing its research program and acting as advisor to the Chief of Navy Personnel.

In 1960, he became director of "Project Talent" where more than 60 measures were developed and administered to one million students in 2,000 secondary schools, with extensive follow-up.

In 1966, Lyndon B. Johnson appointed Dr. Dailey to the President's Commission on Mental Retardation. By the time he joined the FAA in 1968, Dr. Dailey already had developed and applied several dozen "profile" tests to several million persons in the Air Force and Navy, as well as at Texas, Pittsburgh, and George Washington Universities.

The timing was fortuitous. In July of 1968, Department of State officials contacted Dr. Reighard and Dr. Dailey to determine whether they could help stem the rise in hijacking or U.S. aircraft. Dr. Dailey suggested that his previous work on "profiling" might be worth exploring as a possible technique to deal with this growing problem. They met with Acting FAA Administrator Dave Thomas, who was lukewarm to the idea.

However, a break came when Congressman Harley O. Staggers, chairman of the House Committee on Interstate and Foreign Commerce, convened a hearing on air piracy on February 6, 1969. Dr. Dailey's testimony was the key for a Committee mandate ordering the FAA to create a Task Force to deal with aircraft hijacking.

A Dallas psychiatrist had insisted that hijacker motivation was sexually oriented and recommended use of in-flight prostitutes to distract them. Dr. Dailey told Congressman Stagers that aircraft hijacking was simply a matter of "ego gratification."

In January 1971, Dr. Evan W. Pickrel, a widely experienced civil and military researcher, joined the FAA as assistant to Dr. Dailey. He developed a successful program for training pilots on how to abort hijackings. Later, he and Dr. Dailey developed a new system of tests for selection as air traffic controllers. In 1980, Dr. Pickrel succeeded Dr. Dailey upon his retirement.

For his work on developing the "profile," Dr. Dailey received the highest cash award from the FAA, $3,000. In 1972, the Flight Safety Foundation gave him its prestigious Admiral Luis De Florez Award, along with $500 honorarium. In 1975, Texas State University at San Marcos named him Distinguished Alumnus. In 2004, the National Museum of Health and Medicine at Walter Reed Hospital in Washington, D.C. accepted his professional papers, including those dealing with aircraft hijacking.

THE TASK FORCE IS BORN

A cting Administrator Thomas complied with the Committee's order and created the Task Force on Deterrence of Air Piracy 11 days later. He appointed Dr. Reighard as chairman. Since Dr. Dailey had convinced him that this was a multi-disciplined problem, the group would need people from various offices throughout the FAA. These included: Dr. Dailey; Lowell Davis, a safety expert from the Flight Standards Service; Max Collins, like Davis a former military pilot, from the Aircraft Development Service; Joe Blank from the Office of Compliance and Security; John Marsh from the Office of the General Counsel; Lee Jet from the Office of International Aviation Affairs; Bob Friedman from the Office of Management Systems; and, me from the Office of Public Affairs.

Except for Dr. Reighard and Dr. Dailey, the rest of the group did not know one another, and basically were individualistic. However, by the end of its mission, all had become personal friends, an oddity in government.

Dr. Reighard also was something of anomaly. Tall and white-haired, he was basically a shy person. He admitted to me he was uncomfortable even chairing a staff meeting, yet here he was chairing a group that would have a historic impact. And, he was the perfect leader to meld us into a cohesive group.

I was the last person to join the Task Force. After having been an Ohio newspaper reporter for almost 15 years, I became Assistant Director of Information at the Department of Justice in 1967. I had just transferred to the FAA a few months earlier.

WHERE AND HOW TO BEGIN

Almost from the start, the group agreed that our major emphasis had to be to deter potential aircraft hijackers from getting on board. At the same time, we agreed that it would be impossible to stop every attempt because there surely would be fanatics who would give up their lives to accomplish their mission. Therefore, the odds of successful deterrence would be on the ground.

Secondarily, we had to consider what steps could be taken inside the aircraft while in flight. This proved to be a nettlesome problem, but there were some alternatives that could be considered.

This situation placed that usually shy Dr. Dailey in the Task Force's limelight. Combining his previous "profiling" experience with the FAA's own two-stage screening program for civilian pilots, Dr. Dailey engaged in exhaustive research of all possible previous aircraft hijackings to create the most complete data bank on the subject.

Dr. Dailey discovered that some two dozen items seemed to discriminate between innocent airline passengers and past aircraft hijackers who posed as passengers. This included origin and destination of the flight, type of aircraft used, description of airports where aircraft hijacking took place, day of the week and time of the day, operation needs of the aircraft, maintenance needs and their accommodation, weather and other environmental demands, as personnel and equipment interactions.

Crew-hijacker interactions included whether the crew maintained command of the aircraft and control over the situation, and whether the hijacker showed a weapon, took hostages, and/or injured crewmembers. Personal history of aircraft hijackers included age, sex, education, residential situation at the time the ticket was purchased, dress and appearance, mannerisms, operational status, work history, criminal record, etc.

From this, Dr. Dailey developed a list of telltale characteristics that would avoid the dreaded "racial profile" and would be the first of four sequential steps. Those who triggered enough of the "profile" would then be asked to produce valid identification. Next, they would have to pass through the magnetometer to determine whether they were carrying a weapon or an illegal substance. Finally, they would be hand-searched and subjected to an extensive interview.

When Dr. Dailey's "profile" steps were tested at nine airports, no more than 2 percent of all the passengers screened triggered enough of the characteristics to have gone through further screening. At some airports, this dropped to 5-tenths of 1 percent. Also, Dr. Dailey found the "profile" fit 82 percent of past aircraft hijackers.

As an added but unexpected goodie, Dr. Dailey's "profile" also indicated large numbers of drug dealers, various types of law-breakers, illegal aliens, etc. The system was so efficient that drug dealers became convinced the procedure was designed only to catch them.

Dr. Dailey declared that his past experience convinced him that no single-step screening system could be as effective and efficient as a two- or even three-step procedure. He reasoned that this is why a multi-step system is almost universally used in situations similar to airline passenger screening.

According to Dr. Dailey, effective airline passenger screening must utilize information gathered at the boarding gate, at the time of ticketing, and even before ticketing. "With such information at hand, coupled with modern technology, it would be possible to develop a screening system that is both *maximally effective* and *minimally intrusive*," he told the Task Force.

Dr. Dailey complains that "since the system used today is *minimally effective* but *maximally intrusive*, it is a farce because innocent non-threatening airline passengers are subjected to long and unnecessary personal searches."

A federal judge thoroughly examined the original airline passenger screening "profile" soon after it was developed and used, and determined it legal. (This will detailed later on in this book.) "The elements of the 'profile' I developed were revealed to the judge privately during the trial," Dr. Dailey explains. "It is clear that so-called *racial profiles* are neither proper nor legal. They just are out-and-out *racial screening!*"

Dr. Dailey declares the way to put an end to *racial and ethnic screening* is to convince law enforcement officials this violates the Fourth Amendment to the Constitution. "The media should stop referring to *racial profiling* when its true term is *racial screening*," he adds.

With Dr. Dailey's "profile" accepted as Step One, Step Two was to locate a device that would present an effective physical deterrent to boarding the aircraft. This came in the form of an off-the-shelf metal detector called a magnetometer. It was similar to a device the military used in wartime to detect mines.

Dr. Dailey determined that the only available device was one-dimensional, meaning it could not locate a weapon on that part of an airline passenger's body away from the detector. So, he modified it into a U-shaped version that basically is in use today. The one-dimensional device now is the portable one used for additional search.

The proof of Dr. Dailey's approach had to be in field-testing. The original plan called for "secret" tests at three airports – Washington National, LaGuardia in New York, and Miami International. I argued that holding tests at only three locations, and to be "secret" about it, only would lead to negative stories by reporters, blown out of proportion, and inviting adverse speculation. Having been a reporter, I tried to anticipate what the news coverage would be if tests were "secret."

I proposed going to five more airports throughout the country, as well as to San Juan, Puerto Rico, to get a more comprehensive reaction. I also argued for a press conference at each location to openly explain that our mission was to determine how much of the flying public could be *screened out* so we could focus on a *manageable* number. Further, we would make it clear to the public that our system was *not* foolproof, but still could be effective. A reporter later would tell me, "This is the first time I ever hear a government spokesman admit a program was not 100 percent perfect."

Despite my pleas that this approach would be credible with the news media to forestall stories of how reporters "beat" the system, and allay public fears about being "searched," my arguments were rejected by many of the Task Force members. I had the uneasy feeling they felt I would reveal everything and compromise the system, even though I promised we could be as open as possible without breaching security.

There was intense discussion until Dr. Reighard decided my approach was worth a try. In exchange, I said I would develop anticipated questions if the team would help with technical answers. Everyone contributed their input. My goal, which was achieved, was that any Task Force member would speak with a reporter without having to clear with me because we all would be saying exactly the same thing.

Such an approach was unique, and risky, but this agreement seemed to calm their fears. However, when I told my superior about the agreement, he almost went ballistic. The pure bureaucrat that he was, he insisted on having all media calls go through him.

After one meeting, Dr. Reighard asked me to stay behind. With no one else around, he confessed that he was not confident even speaking at one of his staff meetings, at high-level briefings, and even talking with a reporter. I promised to work with him, and we did spend many hours together to make him a more confident communicator. Near the end of the Task Force's work, I came into Dr. Reighard's office one day while he was on the telephone. After he hung up, he said, "I just finished a 45-minute interview with the Voice of America. I really felt good about it, thanks to you."

FIELD-TESTING

Dr. Reighard organized a traveling team, headed by Lowell Davis, that included Max Collins and me. We took along a portable magnetometer, plus a black-and-white videotape recorder that I operated. We worked only with Eastern Airlines.

Our dual purpose was to determine the validity of Dr. Dailey's procedure, and for me to hold a press conference as well as to videotape passengers so we would have a record of their reactions to being screened. We also were trying to determine what percentage of those passengers fit Dr. Dailey's "profile." The results surprised us because no more than 2 percent of passengers we screened exhibited enough of the characteristics to have been detained if the system were in effect. In some cases, the percentage dropped to 5-tenths of 1 percent.

We would fly into a designated city and scout out the airport to agree on how best to set up our equipment. Also, that trip would provide Davis and Collins with the opportunity to explain to gate personnel what we were doing.

When we returned a few weeks later, Davis and Collins would conduct the screening while I did the videotaping. That meant a 12-hour day of setting up the equipment, conducting the testing, meeting with the media, and repacking everything.

At none of the nine airports where I held a press conference did any reporter write about trying to "beat the system" because I admitted the procedure was not fool proof. I was able to gain the confidence of reporters by being as open as possible "within bounds of security." I referred technical questions to Davis and Collins, both of whom were more than up to the task.

When we got back after each trip, we would share our experience with the Task Force. There would be an extensive discussion and analysis so that our traveling team could fine-tune the tests. Even before we visited all nine airports, it became clear that Dr. Dailey's list of characteristics identified no more than 2 percent of the Eastern Air Lines passengers.

Our work with Eastern was a pleasure. We had the full support of Mike Fenello, a senior vice president. My contact was with Jim Ashlock, the 6-feet 8-inch tall director of public relations, likewise an eager supporter.

As I had predicted, we found varying reasons airline passengers took trips to and from different locations. That helped Dr. Dailey tailor his characteristics depending on the airport. Some airport terminals had different configurations, so the magnetometer locations in the security areas would have to be flexible.

When the Task force recommended that airport signs warning of searches be both in English and Spanish, I volunteered to arrange for the latter translation. I contacted the Voice of America, and the agency fully cooperated. After the signs were posted, I received a call from a San Diego airport official. "Are you aware there is Hispanic, Castilian, and Latin Spanish? He asked. "The translation you provided does not work out the same for the different dialects." We quickly printed up different Spanish translations for different areas of the country.

At San Juan, we discovered that the Department of Agriculture maintained an inspection procedure that could act as our screening agent. Other airports had Customs Bureau agents we could rely on.

MORE LESSONS LEARNED

During our LaGuardia Airport test, a New York Times reporter asked me if he could mingle with passengers once they had boarded. I explained that Eastern Airlines had to approve such a situation, but I agreed to help. About 15 minutes later, he returned and snarled at me: "You must have coached these people! They all love your system, especially one passenger who said he only flies Eastern because it is the only airline willing to do something about deterring hijacking." When he described the passenger, I said, "Oh, you mean the delegate to the United Nations. He and I did chat about that, but I did not coach him." The next day, The New York Times story was very positive, and quoted the delegate.

After that first test, I received a call from an Eastern Airlines gate supervisor at LaGuardia. "Do you realize what you have done warning passengers they would have to pass through a metal detector?" he asked. "We have found guns, knives, and even packs of narcotics discarded in potted plants near the boarding gates." Lowering his voice, he added, "You do know we fly a lot of Mafia members between here and Miami, and they may not want to use us anymore. You've got to stop this!"

I quickly called Ashlock, and we agreed these discoveries would make positive news stories. Later, he told me the supervisor was given a special lecture about the merits of our program.

There were other airline officials, however, who were convinced our efforts would ruin their business.

WE'RE IN BUSINESS

Now that the field tests confirmed that we had to deal with a manageable number of "suspects," the Task Force debated several approaches.

One called for publicizing maximum punishment. However, we agreed that this threat would not deter a fanatic, or a group of terrorists. The "Final Report" noted on Page 39 "that there are too many people in too many parts of the world with motivations for violence to argue against expectations that the phenomenon would not only spread but become differentiated in character." *How prophetic those word haves turned out to be!*

Another approach focused on keeping potential aircraft hijackers from boarding a flight. That placed the *major reliance* on Dr. Dailey's list of characteristics. As noted before, this meant focusing on no more than 2 percent of the flying public. We concluded that the odds of dealing with a potential aircraft hijacker on the ground were infinitely greater than when the aircraft was 35,000 feet in the air.

The third approach meant developing an on-board device to immobilize the hijacker without endangering the cockpit crew, flight attendants, and/or passengers. The Task Force and some airlines saws a video about such a device, but its existence became a public guessing game. Suffice it to say the device could be lethal.

Ironically, had such devices been installed in the four "9/11" hijacked airplanes, most, if not all, of the crazed terrorists may well have been able to complete their kamikaze missions.

The Task Force began receiving hundreds of suggestions. Some were realistic, but some were not.

Davis was an expert in aircraft safety. He was responsible for convincing airlines to paint outlines on the outside cabin doors. He discovered that when some airplanes had crashed either onto land or into water, rescuers sometimes had a difficult time figuring out where the cabin door was located so they could extricate passengers and crew.

Putting his professional thinking cap on, he also strongly advocated strengthening the cockpit door. On some of our field-test flights, Davis would point out to Collins and me how some of the cockpit doors either were left open, or were very easy to open. Thankfully, cockpit doors today are very secure. Davis was decades ahead of his time.

A week after "9/11," a Chinese inventor named Zhen-man Lin faxed a proposal to the U.S. Embassy in Hong Kong for what he termed was "a creative hijacking prevention device and system." This was forwarded to the White House. According to him, President Bush announced three cockpit safety measures the following week" that are similar to the ones that (I) proposed." He claimed that the Patent Bureau of China gave its approval to his application.

Among his proposals were "two unidirectionally transparent bullet-proof glass doors" controlling entry into the cockpit; a narcotic spray; a system to lock in the flight course; a special "chase" plane; and, special identification codes and a palm-print device for flight attendants to be able to enter the cockpit.

While our testing had been limited to Eastern Air Lines and its gates, the Task Force wondered whether the system would hold up for other airlines at other airports. Under Dr. Reighard's guidance, the Task Force agreed to propose a final test involving all airlines at one airport. The opportunity to present that came when a meeting of airline executives was arranged to take place in the FAA Administrator's 9th floor conference room.

At the appointed day and time, we all walked into the room to discover not only senior airline officials but also several psychiatrists and psychologists sitting around the large circular table.

Fenello, our "godfather," chaired the meeting. It did not take long for one senior vice president to announce that "we commissioned the Menninger Institute to analyze your program." He went on to say that the results "supported our conclusion that your system will put us out of business because passengers will be afraid to go through the search process before they board their flights."

We had been warned in advance about those "theoretical" studies. We also had been made aware that officials both inside and outside of the FAA felt we were not of sound mind or body. One outspoken critic was the agency's chief psychiatrist. But, we felt if anyone were "far out," it would be the Dallas psychiatrist who recommended the use of on-board prostitutes to distract aircraft hijackers.

We were prepared. To his credit, Fenello allowed his colleagues to vent their emotions, knowing we could address each concern. Then, he called on Dr. Reighard and Dr. Dailey to detail the results of our work, especially the field-testing. Despite their excellent presentations, it was obvious their well-chosen words fell on deaf ears.

Finally, Fenello focused on potential passenger fears. He noted that since we had worked with Eastern, the airline that once had been the most hijacked now was the least. Pausing dramatically, he said, "During the field tests, Dave Brown videotaped passenger reaction. Almost without exception, passengers were willing to be searched because it meant at least the government was trying to do something positive. We also have copies of a New York Times article that proved it."

He paused for a moment, looked around the table, and asked:

"Would you like to see some of those videotapes now?" There was silence. "Are there any questions or further discussion?" Again, there was silence. "Do I take that to mean the FAA has your approval to equip an entire airport with magnetometers and apply the list of Dr. Daily's characteristics?" Everyone nodded in agreement.

The New Orleans airport was designated as the site for the comprehensive test. That would be sink or swim; it was all or nothing.

There was no doubt this meeting was the crucible of our efforts. Had it not been for Fenello's strong support, Dr. Reighard's masterful leadership, and Dr. Dailey's faith in his characteristics, all of our work would have been for naught. We believed in the program, but we had to convince airline executives to believe in it too.

HOPE FOR THE BEST,
BUT PLAN FOR THE WORST

As we had done in the past, Davis, Collins, and I made an inspection trip to New Orleans to make the necessary arrangements for the final all-inclusive test. Working with one airline at one gate was one thing; coordinating the characteristics and the magnetometer for an entire airport was something else. Then, there was the expectation of extensive news media coverage. If we failed, the media would make sure the world knew about it.

The plan was to have our traveling team, plus Dr. Dailey, fly down to New Orleans on a Monday to brief officials on the results of our field testing, as well as introducing them to the characteristics. Dr. Reighard and others would join us later.

We scheduled a news conference for early Thursday afternoon after reporters had a chance to see all the gates in operation with our system. Although we had enjoyed overwhelmingly positive news coverage during the field-testing stage, I still was uncertain how this event would play out. As it turned out, things would not be smooth.

While I was on the telephone working on the New Orleans arrangements, my immediate boss, John Leyden, called me into his office to say our overall boss had noticed that one columnist was vehemently ridiculing our program. "The boss wants you to do something about it," Leyden said.

I had seen his columns, but of more than 200 articles we had documented, his and 5 others were the only negative ones. But, orders were orders.

The first thing I did was determine how many newspapers carried his column – three. I tallied the circulation of those three papers. Next, I counted the circulation of the other 200 stories. I wrote down those figures and showed them to Leyden and argued that we should not be concerned about that one columnist. "I have my orders, and you have yours," Leyden said, although not too convincingly. "OK," I responded.

The columnist worked out of an office in the National Press Building, not far from our facility. I called and invited him over, offering to give him a special briefing. When he showed up, I went over the entire program, and even added a few tidbits not previously known. He thanked me and left. Within days, he wrote another column – worse than any of his others. I showed that to Leyden, who just shrugged. In turn, we took it into our overall boss, who glowered at me.

I made a reservation for the same Monday morning flight to New Orleans my Task Force colleagues would be taking. I also alerted local and national news media outlets that I would be available that evening.

On the previous Friday, that glowering boss called me into his office and said I could not be spared on Monday, but I could leave the following day. However, he added that I would have to be back in the office by Friday morning. Davis, Collins, and I had planned to take annual leave that Friday and spend a long weekend in the "Big Easy" with our wives to unwind.

I did not realize I was so valuable. My civil service rank – lowest of all the Task Force Members – certain did not reflect that.

While sitting at my desk on Monday, I decided that if I were being punished for that columnist incident, that only could hurt the Task

Force effort. The only telephone call I received all day reinforced my hunch.

The call was Davis. He said a very irate Ike Papas, who reported for the CBS/TV program "The Evening News With Walter Cronkite," was ticked off because I was not in New Orleans to brief him. I certainly could not tell him I had been bureaucratically ordered to stay behind.

I called Papas at his hotel and apologized. I explained I had been detained because of an unexpected "emergency" situation that required me to remain in FAA headquarters. I promised to make it up to him when I would arrive Tuesday morning. "You had better be here, or my Thursday piece will not be one you like," he growled. I did not relish the prospect of being the scapegoat for a negative story on national television.

After we hung up, I called Davis back and told him what happened. When the Task Force was first formed, Davis was my major critic. He had been a Navy pilot and apparently had a run in with the Public Affairs officer. However, after he saw the results of the first press conference, he changed his mind and we became close friends. The same went for Collins. We made an effective trio.

"Please show Papas some behind-the-scenes stuff that no one else has seen but that will not compromise security," I pleaded. "He can crucify us. I trust your judgment on how to handle this. Lowell, my career is in your hands now."

THE BIG DAY APPROACHES

When I finally met Papas on Tuesday morning, I said, "Lowell Davis knows more about this project than anyone else. You are in good hands. If you want me to tag along, I will. But, if not, I understand." Papas looked at me and said, "I'll see you on Thursday," and waved goodbye.

For the next two days, I would run into Papas, but we merely traded helloes. I was too busy taking care of the growing number of reporters who began showing up. I assured them that they could interview Davis, Collins, Dr. Reighard, or Dr. Dailey without me around. That astonished some veteran reporters.

The news people were free to go from gate to gate. I had coordinated with my counterparts at various airlines so they could send the same message as ours.

The Thursday press conference was scheduled for early afternoon, in time for the evening television news programs and the next day's morning newspapers. As I was finalizing arrangements, I felt a tap on my shoulder. "Are you Dave Brown of the FAA?" he asked. "Yes," I replied. "Can I help you?" "I'm with the Huntley-Brinkley program on NBC/TV, and I just wanted to introduce myself. I realize I did not let you know I was coming, but I hope that is not a problem." Not a problem at all, I said to myself. I asked him if there were anything I could do for him, but he thanked me and went on his way.

Suddenly, I realized that the two major national evening network television networks – CBS and NBC – now were covering the event. Either we were going to make it big on the evening news, or we would suffer public humiliation.

THE FAT IS IN THE FIRE

I alerted my Task Force colleagues and my airline counterparts. There was nothing more than I could do. Well, I admit I said more than just a little prayer.

The press conference went well. Everyone said the right thing and gave the right answers. The field test numbers were reinforced here. As the press conference broke up, Papas came over to me and said, "I'm going to do my wrap-up right where you are standing, but I don't want you around. Just be sure to watch the show." Ouch, I thought.

My bigger problem was that I would have to be on the return flight to Washington at the time all the television news shows aired. So, I immediately called Leyden to alert him. On a huge leap of faith and a hunch, I called a friend who was the public relations aide to Transportation Secretary John A. Volpe. "I think the Secretary ought to be watching too," I suggested. My last call was to my wife, asking her to watch also.

My wife greeted me at the door with a big smile when I finally got home at 8 p.m. "How did you manage to get such great coverage?" she asked. "Nothing to it," I lied. "Honestly, how was the CBS report? That had me really worried. I thought he would kill us." "Well, he did a very good story," she replied. I slept soundly that night, but I was jealous of my colleagues who would be living it up in New Orleans.

On Friday, Leyden said he had seen the coverage and congratulated me. I never heard anything from the boss. While Dr. Reighard recommended awards for all of us, all I received was a notation that read: "This was what we expected of you."

A NOT-SO-BRIEF BRIEFING

All I did on Friday was clip New Orleans stories for the scrapbook. Lunch was lonesome. The only telephone call I received came late in the day from that aide to Secretary Volpe. "He wants to see the Task Force in his office Tuesday morning at 10," he said. I gulped, almost afraid to ask: "Any idea what it is all about?" He paused, then replied with a chuckle: "He saw both the CBS and NBC programs and wants to know how we got more than two precious minutes of airtime on the major news shows for a program he never was briefed on. Nice going!"

I phoned Dr. Reighard's hotel room and asked him to call me back at home that evening. Dr. Reighard basically was a no-nonsense person, so I decided to string him along a bit. "Secretary Volpe wants to see the Task Force in his office Tuesday morning at 10!" I said sternly. The pause I expected came. "What's that all about?" he asked. Again I paused, and then repeated what the aide had told me. Dr. Reighard laughed heartily and said, "I'll check my calendar to see if I can fit it in. Nice going." He had been my staunchest supporter thought the program.

Secretary Volpe gave us an entire hour for the briefing, a rarity. The only interruption came when a Navy officer, on temporary assignment to his staff, came in with some paperwork for him to sign. The Secretary looked up and said, "Unless this is some from the White House or Capitol Hill, I do not want to be disturbed!" I found out later that officer was his son.

BUREAUCRACY AT ITS WORST

With the New Orleans event a success, the Task Force recommended that the FAA establish a permanent office for airport security. We hoped we would become the nucleus of that new group so our work would have continuity. While the agency did create an Office of Air Transportation Security in August 1970, it "hired" only Lowell Davis and Joe Blank. The rest of us went back to our previous duties, but from time to time, we were asked to brief various officials.

Dr. Dailey and I respectfully submit this was the first in a series of bureaucratic bungling that might have prevented all or part of the "9/11" tragedies.

Despite the publicity about our work, airlines were slow to implement Dr. Dailey's characteristics as the first step in a proper sequential system. In addition, they had problems hiring qualified people to operate the magnetometers.

In subsequent years, the sequence was changed to having *every* airline passenger first go through the magnetometer regardless of whether they triggered any of the characteristics. This flies in the face of our conclusion that if enough of Dr. Dailey's characteristics justify further scrutiny, "it would eliminate the need to search all passengers." (P.57 of the Final Report)

As a result, national and international aircraft hijackings continued, albeit at a slower pace. Yet, the new Office slowly but surely shifted away from the sequence the Task Force has carefully developed. Passenger screening became haphazard.

DR. DAILEY'S LIST
PASSES LEGAL MUSTER

One of the issues the Task Force addressed early on dealt with protecting the civil rights of the flying public while applying proper screening techniques. The group briefed the American Civil Liberties Union on its procedure, and gained its approval on the assurance that the list of characteristics would not identify potential aircraft hijackers on the basis of race, creed, skin color, etc. (Final Report, P.9)

More importantly, the procedure was validated by a May 14, 1971 decision in the Fourth Amendment to the Constitution case of the *United States of America versus Frank Lorenzi Lopez. (328 F. Supp. 1077)* The hearing was held in the U.S. District Court for the Eastern District of New York.

This landmark decision contrasts with what is currently taking place. Judge J. Weinstein ruled that Dr. Dailey's procedure "…is unusual in that it provides statistics showing the precise probabilities involved…The procedure, as designed, operates on *purely objective criteria.*" (P. 1097) (*emphasis added*) He went on state that "the approved system survives constitutional scrutiny *only by its careful adherence to absolute objectivity and neutrality.*" (P. 1101) (*emphasis added*)

The Federal American Law Reports of 1973 agreed that Dr. Dailey's system "which employed *in progression the profile, magnetometer, interviews, and finally a weapons frisk, was constitutional.*" (P. 7) (*emphasis added*)

The *Lopez* decision actually turned on a technicality, but it proved that the system's sequence had to be maintained.

According to the court decision, Lopez and his fellow traveler, Ernesto Perez Gonzalez, were about to board a Pan American Airways flight out of JFK International Airport headed for Puerto Rico on November 14, 1970 when a gate agent believed they fit enough of the "profile" to be detained by U.S. Marshals stationed there. In addition, the two activated the magnetometer.

When Lopez and Gonzalez refused to produce identification, the marshals asked them to go back through the metal detector. They again set it off. The marshals then took them into a private area and "patted" them down, looking for whatever set off the magnetometer. Although Gonzalez had been carrying a small blue bag, the marshals determine nothing in it was suspicious. However, they found a plastic envelope under Lopez's clothing that turned out to contain heroin. He was arrested and later indicted. Gonzalez was absolved.

Lopez's attorney asked the District Court to reject the heroin as evidence. The defense argued that the airline's service manager, on his own initiative, had issued a memorandum four months earlier allegedly to "update" Dr. Dailey's list of characteristics. The judge concluded that the service manager "eliminated one of the fundamental characteristics of hijackers Dr. Dailey described during *in camera* testimony ... (and) added one (that) introduced an ethnic element...raising serious equal protection problems. An added criterion called for individual judgment." (P. 1001)

Judge Weinstein concluded that "the effect of these changes was to destroy the essential neutrality and objectivity of the approved profile." (Ibid)

In ordering the seized packet of heroin suppressed as evidence, the judge stated that the approved anti-hijacking system "can be a valuable and effective method of protecting millions of air travelers from the threat of violence and sudden death in the air." (P. 1102)

The 1973 Federal American Law Review noted Judge Weinstein's conclusion that "even the use of the magnetometer might be an objectionable intrusion were it not accompanied by an antecedent warning from the profile indicating a need to focus particular attention on the subject." (P. 8) "Had the decision to stop and frisk (Lopez and Gonzalez) been made solely on the basis of activating the (magnetometer), the court might have reached a different result." (P.9)

The Review also noted that in *People v. Erdman (1972) 69 Misc 2d 103, 329 NYS2d 654,* the court found there had to be "reasonable grounds to sustain a belief that a passenger about to board an aircraft was armed or constituted a danger, or even created a substantial possibility of danger…(or) a search of the passenger (would violate) his rights under the Fourth Amendment to the Constitution." (P. 12)

At the same time, The Review cited the famous case of *Terry v. Ohio (1968) 392 US1, 201* that concluded limited search could be permitted under "reasonable grounds." (P. 13)

PROFILE PERPLEXITY

The Council on Foreign Relations published a paper titled: "Terrorism Q&A" in 2003. One of the questions was, "Do suicide terrorists fit a common profile?"

This paper noted that there have been many instances in which attackers willingly gave up their lives: "The kamikaze attacks of Japanese pilots during World War II showed a willingness to use suicide as a weapon." The "9/11" attacks on the World Trade Center and the Pentagon sometimes were called kamikaze efforts.

However, the paper noted that "the profile of suicide attackers now requires revision."

The lead editorial in the March 11, 2003 issue of the New York Times noted that the Transportation Security Administration "is developing a sophisticated screening system designed to identify travelers who may pose a terrorist threat. It is a worthy goal – one ordered up by Congress – but the creation of a highly intrusive federal surveillance program raises serious privacy and due process concerns, which the government needs to address is a forthright manner."

The Task Force anticipated that the original "profile" would have to be flexible enough to be adapted to evolving terrorists activities. But, there is the danger that the "profile" can be misused to the point where a passenger's civil rights can be violated. Witness what took place on Delta Flight 442 in August of 2002.

According to a story in The Philadelphia Inquirer, the plane was en route to Philadelphia from Atlanta when a passenger began looking at other passengers' luggage. Two U.S. air marshals rushed back from the first-class seats to investigate and warned passengers to stay in their seats. The unruly man did not comply and was restrained.

The marshals sat the man down next to a passenger later identified as Dr. Bob Rajcoomar, a native of India but a well known private physician. He did not want to remain in his seat, so a flight attendant moved him to one of the first-class seats belonging to one of the Marshals.

When the plane finally landed, and Philadelphia police took the unruly man into custody, one of the marshals rushed back to his seat and ordered Dr. Rajcoomar to put his head down and place his hands over his head, according to the story. Dr. Rajcoomar then was rushed off the plane, taken to an airport police station, and jailed. "During detention," the article reported, he said, "I never was asked anything except my name, address and Social Security number." When he asked why he was being held, he said he was told that one of the marshals "didn't like the way you looked at us." Dr. Rajcoomar finally was released three hours later without an explanation.

From all available information, neither the unruly passenger nor Dr. Rajcoomar fit any of the "profile." Therefore, the cabin crew should have dealt with that situation.

The Task Force went to great lengths to ensure that Dr. Dailey's "characteristics profile" did not become a "racial profile." As noted before, Judge Weinstein ruled that Dr. Dailey's list of characteristics did not violate anyone's civil rights.

IN-FLIGHT DEFENSES

The Task Force openly admitted in press conferences and during reporter interviews that there was no system that could *totally* prevent potential hijacker terrorists from boarding a flight. In their February 1975 article in "American Psychologist," Dr. Dailey and Dr. Pickrel analyzed 30 aircraft hijackings between 1970 and 1971, and concluded that *87 percent would have been stopped at the boarding gate if available procedures had been mandatory, but they only were voluntary at the time.*

What could be done to control the situation once hijackers took, or tried to take, control of the aircraft once it was airborne?

First, a study of successful efforts at thwarting in-flight hijacking situations was shared with airlines for training purposes.

Second, a command center at FAA headquarters was established and staffed with security experts to help the aircraft crews as much as they could. However, by the time the center was in place and operating, aircraft hijackings dropped to almost nothing by the last quarter of 1972.

Third, there were recurring calls for armed air marshals. However, the Task Force felt those marshals only could be used on selected flights because there were just not enough of them to do otherwise.

And, fourth, there currently is a program to train cockpit crew members on how to use firearms. The Task Force did not support such an effort, and currently many cockpit crew members refuse to carry weapons in flight.

THE AIR MARSHAL ISSUE

When pressure began building for use of armed air marshals, the Task Force was aware that some foreign nations, especially Israel, were using such a procedure. However, after much discussion, we concluded that using armed air marshals on U.S. aircraft posed more problems than it solved.

We determined that airlines such as Israel's El Al had a limited number of flights, so armed guards in those situations was a plausible procedure. We also were aware that those guards had orders to shoot to kill, even if that meant harming innocent passengers. We were not convinced the same results would be acceptable on U.S. air carriers. Besides, Israel was on constant alert against Arab terrorists.

While bullets might not protrude through the cabin and reduce air pressure, they might damage the electrical systems. But, that damage could be, and now has been, corrected through modern technology.

Another question that arose concerned whether armed air marshals should be in uniform, as they are in some foreign nations, or should they be dressed like any other passenger. Also, how many marshals should be on flights? If there are not enough armed air marshals on every flight from every airport every day, Dr. Dailey and I submit that terrorists could easily determine which flights were not thus protected.

Also, should those marshals be former or retired military or law enforcement personnel? And, should they be recruited from other federal agencies?

THE FORT DIX FIASCO

In 1971, President Richard M. Nixon ordered the training of military volunteers at Fort Dix, NJ to be a test cadre of air marshals.

By that time, I had transferred to the News Division of the parent Department of Transportation, but I was "volunteered" to coordinate with the military to hold a major press conference when the initial training ended. My boss, Al Sweeney, said I had the ideal credentials. Not only had I been an Ohio newspaper reporter for nearly 15 years before becoming Assistant Director of Information of the Department of Justice during 1967-69 prior to joining the FAA, and had directed media relations for the Task Force between 1969-70, but I also was an Army Reserve office with a mobilization assignment in the Pentagon.

I called Dr. Reighard to alert him as a courtesy.

My military counterpart and I carefully worked out the media strategy. Since the military wanted to downplay its role, I would conduct the press conference. The media would be given demonstrations of various approaches to deal with hijackers while the aircraft was in flight. We both agreed to be as circumspect as possible about the military's role, only describing their training in generalities.

Since Fort Dix was not far from New York City, we drew a great deal of interest not only from the press in the "Big Apple" but also from national and local media. I thought this is déjà vu New Orleans. And, it almost turned out that way.

On the appointed day, after the media had seen the demonstrations, I began the press conference by introducing civilian and military dignitaries. After some opening statements, we took questions from the reporters. As with the Task Force, we had coordinated responses for consistency. We explained that we would be as open as possible within the bounds of security.

Suddenly, a top Department of Transportation official, whom I had previously briefed about this program, seemed to appear out of nowhere. He headed straight for me, and it was obvious he wanted to take over the podium.

At first, all seemed to go well. He handled the first few questions expertly, and I began to relax. When one reporter quizzed him about the type of men the air marshals were, he suddenly turned to me and said, "I think it would be helpful if we would introduce a couple of them."

I literally went into shock! My military counterpart and I had agreed not to reveal their presence because at that point there only were a handful of them fully trained. Identifying them would knock them out of the program because they now would be widely known.

I did not have any choice but to motion two of them forward. They seemed very embarrassed. My military counterpart was fuming, but I just shrugged my shoulders. He knew I too had been taken by surprise.

But there were to be more shocks in the offing.

"While these men will be armed, they will be using special ammunition that will not endanger the aircraft," the official announced. Ouch! My military counterpart and I had agreed not to mention the special bullets in their weapons.

The official told the two air marshals to display some of those bullets. My military counterpart glowered at me worse than before, but all I could do was shake my head from side to side. I never dreamed the official would make such a blunder.

Thankfully, the press conference ended. The official basked in the glow of live coverage. Finally, my military counterpart came over to me and said, "I think it went rather well, considering you will not be welcome on this base ever again, and your civil service career probably is over." But then, he put his hand on my shoulder and said, "Well, at least when you get sandbagged, it's done by top brass."

I called Sweeney first, and then Dr. Reighard, and repeated what had taken place. I also told them that several reporters came up to me afterward, upset that I had not identified the air marshals and had not mentioned the special ammunition. Well, I thought, maybe they'll use those bullets at my firing squad.

However, I did literally shoot myself in the foot.

In addition to the two now revealed air marshals, there were several others who conducted some of the demonstrations. I asked the reporters not to show the men's faces in their photographs. However, we did not have enough air marshals on hand, so I asked a civilian to join in. Later, when I began the press conference and introduced the civilian officials, he was one of them. Unfortunately, a sharp-eyed reporter spotted my gaffe.

I told Sweeney I fully expected to be castigated in the following day's coverage. Luckily, the reporter did not include my mistake in her story. I called her first to apologize, then to thank her for not humiliating me in print. "I really thought about using it," she said, "but I knew you were surprised by that official. I figured you had suffered enough for one day."

Perhaps I got my just desserts later, because the small FAA plane that flew me back to Washington ran into some serious air turbulence. I am not the greatest of air travelers, so by the time we landed, I felt very queasy, and just made it to a nearby rest room.

I did not support using armed air marshals on U.S. flights. However, when the President orders something to be done, it gets done. In his book "Sky Pirates," Jim Arey described the air marshal program as "the best interim solution." (P. 273) It was not a sensible solution as far as most of the Task Force was concerned. And, it could not be interim, because once you start a government program and the flying public knows about it, you cannot shut it down. Ironically, the air marshal program was reduced to very low levels, only to be expanded greatly.

Commercial airline pilots now are being offered firearms training as a result of the Homeland Security Bill signed into law in late fall of 2002. Ironically Transportation Security Administration Director James Loy and some airline industry officials are not very supportive. A November 2002 AllSafe Defense Systems news release wondered why armed air marshals would be needed if the cockpit crew had their own weapons.

THE AIR MARSHAL MYTH MATH

By the FAA's own reckoning, tens of thousands of commercial passenger flights depart from more than 500 airports throughout the country each day. Some are non-stop, and some are multi-stop ones. In 2002, the agency's Bureau of Transportation Statistics reported that "Aircraft Revenue Departures" ranged from 677,000 to 878,000 per month. "Traffic statistics for small certified air carriers and commuter air carriers are not included," according to a footnote. The data also did not include military or commercial cargo flights.

The obvious question is this: If we cannot have armed air marshals on board every flight from every airport every day, which flights will they cover? **There were no armed air marshals on any of the "9/11" terrorist-controlled flights!!!**

A Newhouse News Service online article by Miles Benson in May 2002 quoted John J. Nance, an airline safety expert, as stating "it would take an army of 100,000 (armed air marshals) to adequately guard daily flights in the United States." Benson also observed that "in 1971, air marshals arrested 18 individuals aboard airlines, but in that same year, a gunman diverted an American Airlines Boeing 747 to Havana despite *three air marshals and an FBI agent being on board. (emphasis added)*

The article further noted that after "9/11," law enforcement personnel were borrowed from such Federal agencies as the National Park Service, the Fish and Wildlife Service, and the Postal Service.

According to the article, "The government said it was placing two or more air marshals aboard every flight in and out of Washington's Reagan National Airport." *However, none of the "9/11" kamikaze flights originated from that airport!*

American Airlines Flight 11, a Boeing 767 with five terrorists aboard, took off from Boston's Logan Airport and crashed into the North Tower of the World Trade Center. United Airlines Flight 175, also a Boeing 767 that likewise took off from Logan with five terrorists aboard, crashed into the South Tower. American Airlines Flight 77, a Boeing 757 with five terrorists aboard, took off from Washington Dulles International Airport and crashed into the Pentagon. And, United Airlines Flight 93, another Boeing 757 with four terrorists aboard, took off from Newark International Airport but crashed into the Pennsylvania countryside.

According to statistics in Jim Arey's book, the last time a hijacked airplane left Logan was on August 14, 1969. The last time a hijacked airplane left Newark was on August 19, 1970. There is no record of any hijacked airplane having used Dulles.

The Newhouse article also noted: "The government and the airline industry want to persuade potential hijackers that marshals could be present aboard any flight. But, there aren't enough of them to cover every flight."

The Task Force reached that same conclusion more than three decades ago; yet, there is pressure to create an army of air marshals! Trying to out-think potential aircraft terrorist hijackers, coupled with random searches, is like assuming that eventually you will win the Lottery.

The Los Angeles Times, in a January 14, 2002 article, noted that "on Sept. 11, (air marshals) were in the wrong planes, assigned to selected high-risk international flights not domestic flights like the transcontinental routes targeted by Al Qaeda."

A New York Times article of September 2, 2003 reported that

"Tom Ridge (Secretary of the Department of Homeland Security) said that 5,000 law enforcement officers who work at immigration and customs would be trained to work as federal air marshals so they could be shifted to airliner duty when the department believed that the hijacking threat was high."

The L.A. Times article claimed "it would take 20,000 marshals or more – men and women – who usually work in teams – to cover the 30,000-plus daily flights in the United States, security experts and former government officials said. Such a program could easily cost more than $10 billion a year."

With armed air marshals and armed cockpit crew members hopefully not firing at each other during an airborne terrorist attack, the Final Report noted "as Task Force members also viewed with concern 'cops and robbers' approaches in the skies, they turned full attention to on-the-ground deterrent mechanisms." (P. 34)

The lead editorial in the June 26, 1985 USA Today newspaper warned "we must be cautious about packing airplanes with armed air marshals trained to quell terrorists."

The L.A. Times article also quoted O.K. Steele, who headed the FAA's security branch in the early 1990s, "and others familiar with the history of the program as not aware of any instance in which federal air marshals foiled a hijacking."

AIR MARSHAL PROBLEMS

At one time, there were 1,200 air marshals, but the shrank to only a few dozen stationed at 21 locations around the country prior to "9/11" because budgetary cuts over the years decimated their ranks.

Being an air marshal is not the cushy job most people think it is.

A publication by the U.S. Marshals Service, The Monitor, quoted one of the original air marshals – Louie McKinney -- as saying, "I did it for two years. At first, they'd put me on a Pan American flight from Dulles Airport to London, and I'd sit in the back of the plane and watch what was going on. We'd get there and then I'd turn around and come right back. After three or four flights, I was assigned to the ground at Washington National Airport. I liked this much better."

The Review, published by the Defense Supply Association, noted in its September-October 1971 that boredom was a serious problem. "Among a marshal's problems during long periods in the air (are) looking at the same movies and having to deal with garrulous passengers. He has to keep himself constantly alert to any eventuality."

While many flights carry two air marshals – a man and woman if possible – a jumbo jet like a Boeing 747 requires many more because there is a second deck. One would have to assume they have to keep in touch with one another, and that could be a tip-off to a potential hijacker.

The life of an air marshal mirrors that of a cockpit crewmember and/or a flight attendant involving layovers in far away cities. It also means like cockpit crewmembers and/or flight attendants, air marshals would be limited to their amount of flying time.

If air marshals are on a B-747, they have to keep in touch with one another. A professional terrorist could easily realize who was talking into his or her sleeve, who had an earpiece with a curly Q cord, or who was passing notes to flight attendants.

Air marshals have to rotate flights lest they be seen on the same ones. That also means this is not a 9 to 5 job; they would have to fly at all hours on all days of the week, including holidays. Certainly, this would put a strain on persons with families.

True, air marshals are rotated between air duty and ground duty. But, we respectfully submit that could lead to being "a jack of all trades but a master of none." It means recurring training, both in weapons efficiency and aircraft knowledge.

An article in the June 23, 2002 issue of USA Today reported "the government has cut training for federal air marshal applicants and put new hires on flights without the advanced marksmanship skills the program used to demand." It also quoted an unnamed source as saying "many proficient marshals are reluctant to team with marshals who haven't passed the advanced marksmanship test."

If that were not enough, The Washington Post of June 19, 2003 reported that "air marshals want to leave the Transportation Security Administration in favor of the new Bureau of Immigration and Customs Enforcement." The August 10, 2003 issue of the Miami Herald reported hat minority air marshals claim they get unfair treatment.

Then, there are mundane problems, such as which hotel to stay at during a layover. Per diem allocations are not in the Four Seasons range. Flight crews know where to stay for the best price. So, that is an added cost for the air marshal program.

Meals on board flights? First-class seat versus coach? Incidental expenses? Someone has to pay.

U.S. Senator Kay Bailey Hutchison of Texas introduced legislation on September 12, 2001 to add $1 dollar to the cost of a domestic flight ticket to help defray such expenses.

Then, there is the added cost of extensive background checks on air marshal candidates, plus the comprehensive training they receive.

Click on to SkymarshalOne@Yahoo.com for a home page titled: "Welcome to Aviation Sky Marshal." (Time magazine, among other publications, tried to substitute that term for air marshal, but it really never caught on.) It offers discussions on "how to improve domestic and international air travel" through "sky marshal volunteers." It stated that "flights are now manned by Federal Air Marshals, as well as qualified skymarshal volunteers."

A Federal Air Surgeon's Medical Bulletin was headlined "Bogus Sky Marshals." It cautioned that several private schools in the FAA's Western-Pacific Region were offering courses to train "sky marshals" and "inflight armed security guards." The Bulletin stated emphatically that those schools were not FAA-sanctioned. Legitimate air marshals were trained only by the FAA in those days.

Even though some foreign nations openly have armed air marshals on flights, some of them are not wholeheartedly in favor of this use.

An online version of a BBC broadcast on December 1, 2002 reported that "the proposals (in England) have been greeted with caution by airlines, who stressed that having guns on planes could pose more of a risk than the initial threat."

The broadcast also quoted a spokesman for Virgin Air Lines as saying, "Since 11 September, our focus has been on two areas – strengthening and protecting the security of the flight deck, and enhancing screening and profiling passengers and baggage."

That is what the Task Force concluded more than 30 years ago!

The basic problem expressed over and over again can be summed up in a quote by John Mazor, spokesman for the Air Line Pilots Association, cited in the Newhouse News Service story: "Air marshals are a very important part of the overall strategy. However, everybody recognized that there were never going to be enough of them to cover a majority of flights, let alone all of them."

Mazor also stated: "A loaded and fully fueled cargo 747 makes just as good a guided missile as a passenger jet."

An Associated press story in September 2001 quoted Darryl Jenkins, director of The George Washington University's Aviation Institute, as suggesting that "the thought that there might be a sky marshal on a flight will give comfort to travelers."

Dr. Dailey and I respectfully submit that the realization there are **not** armed air marshals on every flight might have just the opposite reaction.

IS ARMING PILOTS A GOOD ALTERNATIVE?

When President Bush signed the Homeland Security Bill into law in late November 2002, it allowed cockpit crew to carry loaded weapons. This was done over the objections of the airline industry as well as Transportation Security Administration Director James Loy, according to the previously cited AllSafe Defense Systems' article.

The cockpit area on most jet aircraft is cramped at best. In flight, the pilot and co-pilot are strapped into their seats facing forward, preventing them from easily turning around to face an intruder unless they unbuckle their restraint straps. How could a pilot or co-pilot be able to draw his or her weapon, unbuckle the straps, and fire accurately without the possibility of damaging cockpit controls? What if the intruder had a hostage? Or, what if there were several terrorists on board who could cause a diversion in the cabin?

An Internet article stated that "it's far more difficult to control a terrorist in a large aircraft cabin than to prevent one from getting through the small door into the cockpit. If pilots are armed, why would sky marshals be needed?" The article went on to conclude that arming commercial aircraft pilots "will cause Al Qaeda to look for softer targets – like unarmed 747's carrying cargo rather than passengers." As has been pointed out, cargo planes have been hijacked in the past.

There also are those who say terrorists might plan to use even more force if they know there could be a gun battle on board.

WHAT MOTIVATES
AIRCRAFT HIJACKERS?

One of the Task Force conclusions was that any "psychological propaganda" had to be realistic. Today's terrorists have computers, and can access a great deal of information from the Internet.

The Final Report pointed out that early aircraft hijackings were "a brief moment of glory and power for a previously ineffectual and unsuccessful individual. A common denominator was the desire for public attention." (P. 44)

People wanting to go to or from Cuba perpetrated most of the early domestic aircraft hijackings. Obviously, the purposed today has changed drastically. The Task Force clearly forecast this: **"...mass hijacking of U.S. aircraft could also be carried out by an organized group in order to achieve terrorist objectives." (emphasis added)** (P. 93) This supports our insistence that had the Task Force been pretty much kept intact, it would have shifted in a high alert gear in the early 1990s.

The Report also noted that aircraft hijackers have taken over, or have tried to take over, all types of aircraft. These ranged from single-engine Cessnas to four-engine B-747s, from private aircraft to commercial, from cargo to military.

When I was a reporter in Circleville, OH in the early 1950s covering the police beat, I asked a desk sergeant why someone would try to rob a bank that had an armed guard and security cameras. He replied: "You just have to think like a criminal." Dr. Dailey and I respectfully submit we have to think like terrorists to deal with them.

From all available data, it appears that men directed all of the reported aircraft hijackings, although a few women were collaborators.

In an article in the April 1975 issue of "Aviation, Space, and Environmental Medicine," Drs. Dailey and Pickrel argued that the reason men were the chief aircraft hijackers was because they were "vigorous adults who appeared capable of carrying out a threat of violence (and) included homesick Cubans, the mentally ill, extortionists, political terrorists, and even fleeing felons shooting their way on board." (P. 424)

In his 1981 book "The Pioneer Heritage," Dr. Dailey said "the aircraft hijacker wants attention. He hijacks the plane to make a splashy demonstration to call attention to himself or some cause. The gratification apparently comes from an act of high drama representing one brief moment of power and glory in a lifetime of failure." (P.175)

The Task Force recognized that since "hijacking attempts are closely related to political concerns, (that) narrowed the number of travelers likely to engage in air piracy, (that) increased the likelihood that a useable hijacker profile might be developed, (that) suggested the possibility of correlation between international events and hijacking frequency projections, and (that) indicated the need to investigate questions of possible conspiracy." (Ibid, P. 38) "...**too many people in too many parts of the world with motivations for violence to argue against expectations that the phenomenon would not only spread but become differentiated in character.**" (emphasis added) (Ibid, P. 39)

How is that for an accurate prophecy?

THE HOOVER VACUUM

With air marshals having jurisdiction in flight, who has jurisdiction when a hijacked aircraft was on the ground? That was a matter resolved in 1972 that had an unusual twist for me.

Attorney General John Mitchell called a press conference to announce an agreement between the Department of Justice and the Department of Transportation on which agency had the responsibility in such a situation. I was invited as an observer since I had worked as an information officer for the previous attorney general, Ramsey Clark, and since I had been the Task Force press officer.

Retired Air Force Lieutenant General Benjamin O. Davis Jr., who had been named Assistant Secretary of Transportation for Civil Aviation Security, would represent that agency.

I noticed a rear door to Attorney General Mitchell's Conference room open and a lone figure appear. He stood there unnoticed, but I realized it was J. Edgar Hoover, the reclusive director of the FBI. I knew that his top aide, Clyde Tolson, almost always accompanied him, but I recalled that Tolson now was very ill.

No one ever spoke to Hoover alone. But, I walked over to him and introduced myself. "Oh, yes, I remember you. How are you?" I had worked with my counterpart in the FBI, Tom Bishop, but the agency never officially listed an information officer. Maybe Bishop had mentioned me to Hoover, but I doubt it.

As we chatted about the historic days of the late 1960s, I asked

Hoover if he had ever met Davis. "No, I haven't," he answered. I offered to correct that, and Hoover agreed. I could sense a hush in the room as reporters suddenly realized whom I had in tow. Once I introduced Hoover to Davis, I melted back into the crowd.

After Attorney General Mitchell appeared, the press conference began. He announced that the FBI would have the ground jurisdiction. Reporters were eager to get quotes from Hoover, even though the media knew that the FBI director had been lukewarm to assigning agents to aircraft hijacking duty.

I do not recall any discussion about which agency would have jurisdiction over international waters. For that matter, what if, for example, a British Airways aircraft had just left JFK International Airport bound for Heathrow Airport near London, and was hijacked by an Americanized Arab in mid-Atlantic?

Despite the *Lopez* decision, there are other court cases that offer differing views of whether airport searches do, or do not, violate the Fourth Amendment to the Constitution.

The "hot potato" involves *random* searches. I was subjected to one in Philadelphia when my wife and I were returning from a vacation in England in 2002. For no discernable reason, I was the only one of 39 passengers singled out for extensive search, although I know I did **not** trigger **any** of Dr. Dailey's characteristics. Had I refused to be searched, the airline had the right to refuse to allow me to board the flight. "Well, we have to search someone on every flight," I was told.

ARE RANDOM SEARCHES
LAWFUL, OR JUST AWFUL?

While there has to be a Plan B for in-flight anti-terrorist procedures, the Task Force was adamant that keeping an aircraft hijacker from boarding in the first place had to be Plan A. But, does that mean random searches should be part of Plan B? As far as Dr. Dailey and I are concerned, the answer is **no**!

Following my Philadelphia experience, I complained to the Transportation Security Administration (TSA). In a January 8, 2003 response, Shelly L. Myers, assistant director of consumer outreach and education, wrote: "A variety of security measures are applied to the baggage and/or persons of passengers (sic) selected through the screening process, including random searches. This random element prevents potential terrorists from 'beating the system' by learning how it operates. Leaving out any one group, such as senior citizens or the clergy, would remove the random element from the system and undermine security. We simply cannot assume that all future terrorists will fit any particular profile."

Hogwash!

If TSA officials had read the Final Report, they would have seen that our field tests confirmed that no more than 2 percent, and in some instances less than one-half of 1 percent, of passengers screened fit enough of Dr. Dailey's list of characteristics to require them to be further investigated.

If TSA officials had read Judge Weinstein's ruling, they would have seen that Dr. Dailey's list, and most especially the *sequence*, were constitutional and did not violate the Fourth Amendment.

What field-testing has been done, and what evidence is there, to support Ms. Myers' assertion that random searches "prevent potential terrorists from 'beating the system?" None!

What evidence is that that "senior citizens or the clergy" fit enough of Dr. Dailey's characteristics to warrant random searches? None!

There is nothing wrong with having all passengers go through the magnetometer, or having their luggage screened. But, Dr. Dailey and I challenge the TSA to show that random searches have resulted in anything other than humiliating innocent passengers.

Judge Weinstein's ruling in *Lopez*, which has not been overturned, states that Dr. Dailey's "profile operates on purely objective criteria independent of race, color, or creed. It is well calculated to winnow out potential skyjackers (sic) while occasioning a bare minimum of inconveniences to a very small percentage of the flying public." (P. 1097)

The TSA's approach seems diametrically opposite of Judge Weinstein's ruling! If the TSA's rationale for random searching is the premise that potential aircraft hijackers will be deterred because they will not know how to beat a system, we respectfully submit it had jut the opposite result during "9/11" when terrorists certainly "beat the system" all the Logan, Newark, and Dulles Airports.

The question is this: Just what system was in place during "9/11" that the terrorists beat? There is evidence that there was some suspicion of some of those terrorists, but once they produced identification, they were permitted to board their flights. Had the Task Force still been in business, as has been stated before, the "system" would have fine-tuned the "profile" and upgraded the magnetometer sensitivity.

How were the terrorists able to board their flights with those "box cutters?" Simply put, the magnetometers were not sensitive enough.

How were five terrorists per flight (four on one flight) able to board when their commonality of characteristics should have raised a high alert?

The Task Force and the TSA agree with one sentence in Ms. Myers' letter: "We simply cannot assume that all future terrorists will fit any particular profile." Check the last sentence on Pg. 39 of our Final Report where we anticipated that eventuality. The difference is that the Task Force would have made the "profile" flexible enough to match current terrorist activity throughout the world.

Dr. Dailey and I are not alone in our disdain for random searches. An Internet posting by Michael Hammerschlag titled "Airline Insecurity" asserts: "By definition, the chance that any single random security breach is an *actual* (sic) terrorist is negligible, since terrorists are so infinitesimal a number."

In a Time magazine essay of March 18, 2002, noted columnist and television panelist Charles Krauthammer was vehement in his denouncement of random searches.

"Random passenger checks at airports are completely useless," the article stated. "Random searches are a ridiculous charade... that not only gives a false sense of security but, in fact, diminishes security because it wastes so much time and effort on people who are obviously no threat. Random searches are being done purely to defend against the charge of racial profiling."

In a response to Mr. Krauthammer's essay, Dr. Dailey wrote: "Racial and ethnic screening can only produce an illegal search." That is what Judge Weinstein also concluded.

In the September/October 1971 issue of "Review," published the Defense Supply Association, H.R. Kaplan's article stated that the Task

Force's proper sequence of airport security does not include random searching. "The program is designed to speed passengers who are unlikely to present danger, and to isolate, with the least possible discomfiture or delay, those presenting a substantial probability of danger," he asserted.

There are those who claim random searches violate the Fourth Amendment. It is a fact that some passengers are detained without having met any of the "profile" as I was. There are those who have had to remove their shoes because one passenger was able to carry a "shoe bomb" on board a flight.

Are random searches merely the result of laxity on the part of screeners? Jim Arey, in his book, states: "…even if your policy were one hundred percent search, after a couple of weeks people would let down and be careless, and there would be some of them that get through." (P.270)

A "Handbook of the Bill of Rights," published in 1968 by the Council on Younger Lawyers of the Federal Bar Association, noted that the Supreme Court of the United States ruled in *Terry v. Ohio, 392 U.S. 1* that the Fourth Amendment does not prohibit personal search **"so long as it was reasonable." (emphasis added)** (P. 28) In this case, a policeman was justified in searching a robbery suspect for a weapon only because it **"might present a danger to himself or to others."**

We respectfully submit that random searches are conducted without *reasonable cause* in the hopes of finding something that "might present a danger to himself or others."

There are those who will argue that confiscating such items as nail clippers or aerosol cans "might present a danger" to the crew and passengers on flight. *There is no evidence that such "weapons" ever have been used in an aircraft hijacking.*

Further, there is an inconsistency from airline to airline, and from airport to airport, as to what "might present danger." A case can be made for "weapons" that never are confiscated, but could be "dangerous."

The Fourth Amendment also deals with "administrative searches." These are described as those made by inspectors "to see that housing, health, and fire codes are obeyed." (P. 29) ***None of those apply to the rationale for random searches.***

In *Camara v. San Francisco, 387 U.S. 523, 534 (1967)*, the Supreme court ruled that administrative searches "when authorized and conducted without a warrant lack the traditional safeguard which the Fourth Amendment guarantees to the individual."

While there are no warrants issued in random searches, those who refuse to submit can be denied boarding. We respectfully submit that amounts to being considered guilty until proved innocent. That would appear to conflict with what most of us believe to be the rules of justice in America.

We further respectfully submit that this tacit permission to be randomly searched is made under the premise that the "9/11" attacks placed this country in a virtual but undeclared state of war that allows extreme security measures to be taken.

Our question is whether such extreme measures justify random searches that have yet to produce measurable results, but which may infringe on an individual's civil rights against improper search guaranteed under the Fourth Amendment.

Would random searches have prevented "9/11?" We respectfully submit that the "9/11" terrorists were so willing to give up their lives that they would have devised a plan to neutralize such searches. Three of the four flights have five terrorists, and misdirection would have been an obvious alternative. Ask any pickpocket about how easy misdirection is easy to accomplish.

Would random searches have deterred those terrorists? Japanese kamikaze pilots in World War II were not deterred by the awesome firepower from American naval guns, even though relatively few of those planes found their marks. We respectfully submit terrorists would react in the same way – even if only a few of them completed their mission, that would be symbolic. As history has shown, the terrorist masterminds were astonished at the total devastation of the World Trade Center's twin towers.

OUR PREDICTIONS WERE IGNORED

With the decline in aircraft hijackings over the past three decades, the FAA and the airlines relaxed their active vigil against this problem per se, and relied on the passive procedure of relying on the magnetometer rather than applying the "profile" first.

The Final Report warned **"that the FAA and the air carrier industry would be well advised to prepare for possible future all-out attacks on American carrier transportation." (emphasis added)** (P. 72)

According to the Final Report, "As part of its interest in providing for possible motivational changes and later escalation of hijacker activity, the Task Force devoted much time to a workable 'contingency plan' for future use (that included) measures for temporary strengthening of anti-hijack techniques already developed, and it outlined procedures for use in situations involving a serious threat to the national security or to air commerce as a whole. The contingency plan objective was to develop a state of preparedness in a partnership of the Federal Government, U.S. air carriers operating under Federal Aviation Regulations, the Air Transport Association, pilots and crewmen organizations, airport managers and applicable law enforcement officers (to) maintain an effective system of civil air transportation in times of emergency." (Pp. 72-73) The Report also noted: "Hanging over every act of air piracy is the possibility of an international incident." (P. 33) And, "Air piracy historically relates to political problems perceived by the hijacker." (P.37)

Also, "The Task Force was aware that mass hijacking of U.S. aircraft could also be carried out by an **organized group** in order to **achieve terrorist activity." (emphasis added)** (P. 93)

However, terrorist acts were heating up in the Middle East during the 1990s, but apparently the FAA and the airline industry did not connect these potential aircraft hijacking dots. Had they read The Report, they would have noticed this: "Recognition that hijacking attempts are closely related to political concerns…suggested the possibility of correlation between international events and hijacking frequency projections." (P. 38)

In his book, Jim Arey concocted a round-table discussion involving actual "players" in the hijacking program. Based on his research, he suggested remarks he felt each one would give:

Dr. Dailey: "But in the evolution of hijacking, the thing is evolving in all directions and we don't know what the future is going to hold. But it is quite probable that it won't be all what we had in the past." (P. 269)

Frank Cardman (director of security for Pan American World Airways): "You can't protect yourself one hundred percent, not against a **quasi-military operation…you can't keep every hijacker in the world off an aircraft.** Security must be flexible." **(emphasis added)** (P. 273)

Benjamin O. Davis Jr.: "Unless the pressure is kept on…vigilance really is going to be that only thing to keep us out of trouble in the future." (P. 278)

Davis: "If you look at world events, you will find that things like hijackings, like assaults against constitutional authority, and the very strong increase in violence itself, come right along together. Hijacking is part of the pattern…Until everybody gets to understand that **mass violence, or violence against large numbers of people and valuable** property, is not going to be acceptable, we stand in danger. What we need is an *attitude* of awareness that we have a continuing problem." (emphasis added (P. 279)

P.O. (unnamed publicity officer): "**We just can't sit around and wait for things to happen. We have to be watching trends and trying to predict what may happen in the future. We have to know not only what the threat is but what it is *likely* to be.**" (**emphasis added**) (P. 280)

Dr. Dailey: "We base our estimates…primarily on the **up-to-date intelligence information we get. We realize that our system has to be changed as the nature of the phenomenon changes.**" (**emphasis added**) (P. 280)

P.O. – "There are a number of things that might cause **a terrible catastrophe. I think it is inevitable.**" (**emphasis added**) (P. 281)

Davis: "(the political activist threat) can be made to happen here by any group of terrorists that considers itself so strongly dedicated to a cause that they think it requires **an attention-getting act**… extremists are likely to be misguided (and) when you get a misguided person, **heaven knows what he may do.**" (**emphasis added**) (P. 282)

Referring to what felt was the consensus of the "group," Arey concluded: "Extremists groups? That *is* the political activist threat… that's what can be made to happen here." (P. 283)

Concern about the potential future attacks was voiced more than three decades ago. To us, it is apparent the FAA and the air carrier industry continued a business-as-usual attitude only until terrorists turned "9/11" into a day of national catastrophe.

Suddenly, panic security reaction set in and has persisted. We respectfully submit that random searches became a knee-jerk panic reaction.

The Task Force was committed to "constant testing of the usefulness of (its) system (of "profile" first, etc.)." (P. 63 of The Final Report) We were fearful that laxity would lead to serious problems, and that certainly became the case. The New York Times of July 9, 1985 headlined a Page 1 story: "Anti-hijack Devices on Hand, But Use is Found Inadequate."

Skyjacking was not just a domestic problem. The Civil Aviation Authority in Canberra, Australia reported in the early 1900s that "even if a nation's airports have adhered to (proper screening procedures), each screening stage is fallible. Within days after Lockerbie, the FAA modified their (sic) Security Programs to ensure total reconciliation between passengers and their luggage. However, the President's Commission on Aviation Security and Terrorists (1990, P. 15) found that FAA inspections in Frankfurt and Heathrow during the following two months revealed violations and erratic application of guidelines and poorly trained and supervised security."

WHO SWITCHED PROCEDURAL GEARS, AND WHY?

If Judge Weinstein concluded that Dr. Dailey's "profile" and the sequence in which it was used were legally sound to form the basis for proper search, why did the FAA put the "profile" second and the fallible magnetometer search first?

If Judge Weinstein concluded that the Task Force properly field-tested Dr. Dailey's "profile" to confirm that no more than 2 percent of the flying public, and in some instances less then 5-tenths of 1 percent, fit enough of the characteristics to be more thoroughly searched, why did the FAA put the "profile" second and the fallible magnetometer search first?

Dr. Dailey and I conclude that over the course of time, the FAA decided it would be easier to rely on the magnetometer. But, that meant *reversing* what the Task Force determined, and what Judge Weinstein concurred in.

Despite the Task Force's objections to armed air marshals because they could not possibly cover every flight from every airport every day, the FAA first used some 2,000 of them, then allowed the ranks to be depleted to around two dozen. Now, the Transportation Security Administration, which took over that program, boosted the numbers back up. Also, the TSA took advantage of improved electronic screening technology.

We respectfully submit that this is like locking the barn door after the horse has been stolen.

RED FLAGS WAVED,
BUT NO ONE SALUTED

In a May 26, 2002 story in The Boston Globe, reporter Ralph Ranalli wrote that the FAA issued a warning to airports and airlines in late 1998 that there might be a terrorist aircraft hijacking at an airport in the eastern part of the United States.

The article stated that according to classified security bulletins the newspaper had obtained, the FAA stressed a "high degree of vigilance against threats to the US (sic) civil aviation from Osama bin Laden's terrorist network." The article further stated that while the FAA had been keeping track of bin Laden and his terrorist group, "the agency never had a credible hijacking threat."

Also, the article noted that "British administration and FAA officials have characterized pre-Sept. 11 intelligence warnings as too broad to defend against."

Five days earlier, The New York Post ran a story by Niles Lathem that alleged the FAA "admitted yesterday it had decided not to order a security alert at the nation's airports despite being warned before Sept. 11 that the man now accused as the '20th hijacker' was in custody."

According to an August 12, 2001 story in the German newspaper Die Welt, "Western secret services knew as far back as 1995 that suspected terror mastermind Osama bin Laden planned to attack civilian sites using commercial passenger planes."

And, in a September 18, 2002 report, the Joint Congressional Committee on Intelligence concluded American had 12 warnings between 1994 and August 2001.

BAD PROCEDURES
CAUSE BAD RESULTS

There does not seem to be any evidence that in warning airports and airlines they should be "vigilant" that the FAA specified how to implement the meaning of that term. We respectfully submit that at the very least the FAA should have urged airports and airlines to fine-tune Dr. Dailey's "profile" and to upgrade magnetometers. Neither procedure would have been difficult to do.

By failing to implement what the Task Force tested and proved correct, we respectfully submit that this was spawned an expensive and ineffective procedure that nearly brought U.S. air travel to its financial knees. This procedure scared off a significant number of would-be passengers for many months.

The White House Commission on Aviation Safety and Security that Vice President Al Gore chaired in the mid-1990s may have exacerbated the situation. In 1996, President Clinton signed into law the legislation recommended by the Commission. Part of the $330 million funded better electronic screening of airline passengers, but the law also created what the American Civil Liberties Union called "a higher level of screening based on race or religion," according to a September 5, 1996 story in the U.S. News magazine. We feel this action was yet another bureaucratic mistake.

The article quoted ACLU Legislative Counsel Gregory Nojeim as stating, "Safety and privacy will not be assured if people are targeted for searches based on incorrect criteria instead of evidence." We contend this reinforces the decision in the *Lopez* case.

Dr. Dailey and I respectfully submit that the government and/or the FAA did not have to find a "smoking gun" to refocus on the no more than 2 percent of the flying public the Task Force identified as potential aircraft hijackers. Instead, by some rationale that escapes us, an improper profile was rushed into action, causing more legal problems than it was supposed to solve.

Calling it a "controversial endeavor," a March 11, 2003 lead editorial in The New York Times noted: "The (TSA) is developing a sophisticated screening system designed to identify travelers who may pose a terrorists threat. It is a worthy goal – one ordered up by Congress – but the creation of a highly intrusive federal surveillance program raises serious privacy and due process concerns, which the government needs to address in a forthright manner."

The editorial described "profiling" as "a rudimentary system designed in the mid-1990s (that) helped airlines flag passengers deserving heightened security." Assuming that the editorial writer was referring to Dr. Dailey's "profile," his list of characteristics was confirmed through extensive field-testing. In addition, Judge Weinstein ruled the "profile" and its first step in a screening sequence constitutional. Further, routine research would have revealed that the system was developed during 1969-70.

Screening checked or carry-on luggage is a good idea. Matching luggage with passengers is a good idea. Almost strip-searching an 80-year-old white-haired grandmother (a neighbor of mine) is not a good idea. Only perfunctorily searching some of the "9/11" terrorists was a horrendous boner!

WHAT GOES AROUND, COMES AROUND

On September 9, 2003, The Washington Post had a Page 1 story announcing development of an electronic color-coding system to classify the potential risk air passengers might pose. It is called Computer Assisted Passenger Pre-screening System II (CAPPS II).

The Transportation Security Administration said the coding is being based in part of city departure, destination, traveling companions, and date of ticket purchase. Did some say this could be déjà vu of Dr. Dailey's "profile?"

The Post reported that most people will be coded Green, presumable meaning they will be given the green light to proceed. Up to 8 percent of passengers will be coded Yellow and will undergo additional screening at the checkpoint as a cautionary measure. Between 1 and 2 percent who qualify for code Red will be stopped from boarding while they will face further scrutiny.

TSA spokesman Brian Turmall was quoted as saying "the system will provide protections for the flying public." In 1972, Assistant Secretary of Transportation for Safety and Consumer Affairs Benjamin O. Davis, Jr. held a press conference following a meeting of top U.S. aviation officials. He told reporters: "The Federal Government as the responsibility, and the obligation to the public, to assure full compliance with (FAA security) regulations and to make certain that they are tailored and strengthened as appropriate to meet future threats."

Dr. Dailey and I respectfully submit any new system, whether CAPPS II or any other, must stand the test of court review. But, how ironic that an electronic "profile" once again is the first step in airport screening.

When the Gore Commission, as it was called, was still deliberating over how to improve airport security, Dr. Dailey wrote to the Vice President that "any security program for civil aviation will have to include search and seizure procedures that have been reviewed by the courts and accepted as being legal under the Constitution." He also pointed out that "profiles (must) maintain adherence to absolute objectivity and neutrality."

So, it remains to be seen whether the well-intentioned CAPPS II meets the tests of "objectivity and neutrality."

Dr. Dailey and I do not take any pleasure in literally saying "we told you so, but no one listened." We are not convinced that given airport security today that terrorists will try this same method again. But, aircraft are not the only modes of transportation that could provide the means for another type of terrorist attack. Having said that, our Task Force only was directed to deal with the airline industry. However, in view of today's circumstances, fuller coordination with other agencies within the Department of Transportation and with the new Department of Homeland Security is a must.

But, as the Final Report pointed out, a system only is as good as the people who operate it. "Human error or carelessness in use of deterrents might permit a hijacker to slip through the course of obstacles.." (P.6)

THE DOOR IS OPENED TO "9/11" LAWSUITS

On September 9, 2003, U.S. District Court Judge Alvin Hellerstein ruled in New York City that families of those killed or injured can sue American Airlines and United Airlines – the two that the terrorists hijacked – the Boeing Co. – maker of the aircrafts – and the Port Authority of New York and New Jersey – which owns the World Trade Center that was demolished in the Kamikaze-style attacks.

The defendants reportedly will appeal his decision.

Judge Hellerstein was quoted in the media as stating "negligent security screening might have contributed to the deaths of 3,000 people." In his decision, the judge asserted. "The aviation defendants controlled who came onto the planes and what was carried aboard. They had the obligation to take reasonable care in screening."

Another portion of the judge's ruling should strike a familiar cord: "Airlines reasonably could foresee that crashes causing death and destruction on the ground were a hazard that would arise should hijackers take control of a plane."

As of this writing, no mention has been made as to whether the FAA would have to share some of the blame. Surely, the issue of screening, especially "profiling," should be raised. There also should be the issue about the lack of sufficient air marshals on those fatal flights if the air marshal program is supposed to be effective.

Some are calling this a landmark case. If so, it should be taken in tandem with the *Lopez* decision.

JUMPING THROUGH HOOPS

The U.S. Senate Republican Policy Committee issued a "white paper" in November 2001 quoting the American Civil Liberties Union (ACLU) as having adopted an official policy in the Spring of 1973 that "oppose(d) the present and previous systems of airport searches because they violate the requirements of the Fourth Amendment." (P. 1)

Compare those remarks with our Final Report of 1978 that clearly stated: "The American Civil Liberties Union has agreed the system does not violate civil rights of passengers." (P. 9, No. 4) That "system" was the one our Task Force developed that focused on Dr. Dailey's "profile" and which carefully avoided any semblance to "racial profiling."

Also, the Committee should have perused the decision in the *Lopez* case in which Judge Weinstein declared: "The approved system (referring to what the Task Force developed) survives constitutional scrutiny only by its careful adherence to absolute objectivity and neutrality." (P. 1101) And, "Properly supervised, it (our system) also is constitutional." (P. 1102)

As noted, Judge Weinstein found that the airline employee who relied on the system added a characteristic that "introduced an ethnic element for which there is no experimental basis." He also noted that a second criterion was added to Dr. Dailey's list that improperly "called for an act of individual judgment on the part of airline employees." (Ibid)

However, the "white paper" quoted the ACLU that "the current practice of searching the persons and belongings of *all* individuals, simply because they wish to board an airplane, is completely inconsistent with Fourth Amendment principles." (P. 2)

The "white paper" cited W.R. LaFave's 3rd edition of his "Search and Seizure" treatise in which he validated our original sequence in which the "profile" was the first step. "Under the original detection scheme, activation of the magnetometer was deemed significant only if the individual passing by the machine had therefore been identified as a 'selectee' by use of the profile." (P. 619)

LaFave also referred to the famous *Terry v. Ohio* case in which the Supreme Court of the United States determined that a policeman could frisk a person if he were convinced it was needed to "protect himself and others from possible danger." (P. 622)

He also cited the case of *United States v. Albarado* in which the court found that "use of the magnetometer alone 'would not serve any valid purpose,' as a high percentage of passengers activate the device even if carrying innocuous items." (P. 636) LaFave concluded that "it by no means follows, however, that the screening authorities should immediately proceed to frisk a person who has activated the magnetometer. Such a procedure would deprive the hijacker detection system of a characteristic which is essential to it being deemed…no more severe (an intrusion) than is necessary to produce 'acceptable results.'" (Ibid) In *United States v. Scott,* LaFave says the Supreme Court ruled that "searches are to be judged by a 'standard of objective reasonableness'." (P.649)

The American Law Reports of 1973 contained a differing view. It cited *United States v. Skipworth* as concluding that "reasonableness does not require that officers search only those passengers who meet (the) FAA personality profile or who manifest signs of nervousness or who otherwise appear suspicious." (P. 20) In *United States v. Cyzewski*, it stated the court found that "airport security measures are reasonable insofar as they permit government agents to determine whether (a) suspect presents (an) immediate danger to air commerce." (Ibid)

In *United States v. Doran*, "airport searches are reasonable where limited in scope to (the) object of (the) antihijacking (sic) program; reasonableness of specific search need not be in any way dependent upon (a) magnetometer 'search' nor on showing of conformity with (the) FAA skyjacker profile." (P. 21) That was balanced with the decision in *United States v. Miner* in which the court concluded that "all airport screening procedures, whether conducted by airline employees or government officials, must pass (the) constitutional test of reasonableness." (Ibid)

In *Shapiro v. the State of Florida*, the court found that "preboarding (sic) searches do not violate (the) Fourth Amendment if conducted for (the) purpose of discovering whether (a) prospective air passenger poses (an) immediate threat to air commerce. (P. 23) And, in *Oishi v. the State of Florida*, the court determined that "probable cause was not requisite to justify (a) search for weapons as part of (a) routine procedure involving every passenger who boarded (a) commercial airline.

Keep in mind that the *Lopez* decision never has been overturned.

THE "OTHER PLANE" THAT HIT A NEW YORK SKYSCRAPER

On Saturday, July 28, 1945, a B-25 bomber crashed into the 79th floor of the Empire State Building. It was not a terrorist attack, but the three-man crew and 11 people working in the building perished.

On that day, New York City was fogged in. Lieutenant Colonel William Smith, the pilot, was headed to Newark, NJ to pick up his commanding officer. For some unexplained reason, he hovered over what is not LaGuardia Airport. The air traffic controller wanted him to land there, but Smith wanted to continue on to Newark.

Although regulations required that planes had to fly at least 2,000 feet over Manhattan, Smith dropped to under 1,000 hoping to get low enough to see the ground. When he was shocked to see skyscrapers all around him, he zigzagged around some of them but could not avoid the Empire State Building. The impact created a fireball.

Although it was a Saturday morning just before 10 o'clock, people often worked a six-day week during World War II. There was a small work force in the offices of what is now known as Catholic Relief Services. They never had a chance.

One of the plane's engines broke loose and catapulted through several walls and went out a window, landing on the roof of a nearby building. The other engine landed on a descending elevator containing two women, but a "slowing device" saved their lives.

Ironically, the Empire State Building was Manhattan's tallest structure at the time. The World Trade Center twin towers held that same distinction prior to "9/11"

EPILOGUE

It has been a painful chore writing even this small a book. Dr. Dailey and I feel the course of history might well have been changed had the original "profile" and sequential system been in place on "9/11."

If so, all those lives would have been spared. There might not have been the incursions of Afghanistan and Iraq and their human toll.

There might not have been the Department of Homeland Security, or the Transportation Security Administration.

There might not have been an era of fear, the likes of which are historically unique for America.

There might not have been international repercussions.

The "what if" question may never be solved.

Dr. Dailey and I feel our story needs to be told here because it has not been told before. As retired government workers, we cringe at how bureaucracy can be overpowering. The Task Force plowed new ground, thinking "outside of the box" as the saying goes. Perhaps that is why its work literally was shelved.

Our prayers go out to those who still mourn. We are among them.

APPENDIX

Entry of the 9/11 Hijackers into the United States

Staff Statement No. 1

Members of the Commission, we have developed initial findings on how the individuals who carried out the 9/11 attacks entered the United States. We have also developed initial findings on terrorists who failed in their efforts to enter the United States. These findings lead us to some tentative judgments on the way the United States targets the travel of international terrorists.

This staff statement represents the collective effort of several members of our staff. Susan Ginsburg, Thomas Eldridge, and Janice Kephart-Roberts did most of the investigative work reflected in this statement.

The Commission was able to build upon a large and strong body of work carried out by many talented public servants at the Department of State, the Central Intelligence Agency, the former Immigration and Naturalization Service, the Department of Homeland Security, and Federal Bureau of Investigation. The American people should be proud of the many extraordinary professionals now serving them. To the extent we have criticisms, they are comments less on the talent available and more on how that talent was used.

As we know from the sizable illegal traffic across our land borders, a terrorist could attempt to bypass legal procedures and enter the United States surreptitiously. None of the 9/11 attackers entered or tried to enter our country this way. So today we will focus on the hijackers' exploitation of legal entry systems. We have handed out a list of the names of 9/11 attackers to help you follow our discussion.

To break down some of al Qaeda's travel problem, view it from their perspective. For most international travel, a terrorist has to have a passport. To visit some countries, terrorists of certain nationalities must obtain a document permitting them to visit – a visa. Finally the terrorist must actually enter the country and keep from getting detained or deported by immigration or other law enforcement officials. Susan Ginsburg, Senior Counsel to the Commission, will begin by examining how the hijackers navigated these stages.

Passports

Four of the hijackers' passports have survived in whole or in part. Two were recovered from the crash site of United Airlines Flight 93 in Pennsylvania. One belonged to a hijacker on American Airlines Flight 11. A passerby picked it up and gave it to an NYPD detective shortly before the World Trade Center towers collapsed. A fourth passport was recovered from luggage that did not make it from a Portland flight to Boston onto the connecting flight, which was American Airlines Flight 11. In addition to these four, some digital copies of the hijackers' passports were recovered in post-9/11 operations.

Two of the passports that have survived, those of *Satam al Suqami* and *Abdul Aziz al Omari,* were clearly doctored. To avoid getting into the classified details, we will just state that these were "manipulated in a fraudulent manner," in ways that have been associated with al Qaeda. Since the passports of 15 of the hijackers did not survive, we cannot make firm factual statements about their documents. But from what we know about al Qaeda passport practices and other information, we believe it is possible that six more of the hijackers presented passports that had some of these same clues to their association with al Qaeda.

Other kinds of passport markings can be highly suspicious. To avoid getting into the classified details, we will just call these "suspicious indicators." Two of the hijackers, *Khalid al Mihdhar* and *Salem al Hazmi,* presented passports that had such suspicious indicators. We know now that each of these two hijackers possessed at least two passports. All of their know passports had these suspicious indicators. We have evidence that three other hijackers, *Nawaf al Hazmi, Ahmed al Nami,* and *Ahmad al Haznawi* may have presented passports containing these suspicious indicators. But their passports did not survive the attacks, so we cannot be sure.

Fifteen of the 19 hijackers were Saudi nationals. There were significant security weaknesses in the Saudi government's issuance of Saudi passports in the period when the visas to the hijackers were issues. Two of the Saudi 9/11 hijackers may have obtained their passports legitimately or illegitimately with the help of a family member who worked in the passport office.

We do not yet know the answer to the question whether the knowledge of these particular clues existed in the intelligence community before 9/11. From the mid-1970s, when terrorists began to launch attacks in the Middle East and Europe, intelligence and border authorities knew that terrorists used forged or altered travel documents. By the 1980s the U.S. government had developed a "Red Book" used to guide and train consular, immigration, and customs officers throughout the world on spotting terrorists. It included photographs of altered or stolen passports, and false travel stamps (also known as cachets) used by terrorist. The importance of training border officials on use of the Red Book is evident from a U.S. government film entitled "The Threat is Real." Here is a brief excerpt:

The U.S. government ceased publication of the "Red Book" by

1992, in part because it had fallen into the hands of terrorist groups, although there continued to be a number of government efforts to provide information about generic forgery detection and document inspection techniques.

Before 9/11, the FBI and CIA did know of some of the practices employed by al Qaeda. They knew this from training manuals recovered in the mid-1990s and from tracking and interrogations of al Qaeda operatives. Some of this knowledge was revealed in individual criminal cases prosecuted in the United States in the 1990s. And yet, between 1992 and September 22, 2001, we have not found any signs that intelligence, law enforcement, or border inspection services fought to acquire, develop, or disseminate systematic information about al Qaeda's or other terrorist groups' travel and passport practices. Thus, such information was not available to consular, immigration, or customs officials who examined the hijackers' passports before 9/11.

Visas

The State Department is principally responsible for administering U.S. immigration laws outside of the United States. Consular officers, a branch of our diplomatic corps, issue several kinds of visas for visitors and for permanent immigrants. In 2000, these diplomats processed about 10 million applications for visitors' visas at over 200 posts overseas. U.S. law allows nationals of certain countries to enter without visas on a reciprocal basis, under the visa waiver program. None of the 9/11 hijackers, however, were nationals of a visa waiver country.

Before 9/11, visa applicants provided their passport and a photograph. A State Department employee checked the passport for any apparent questionable features. A consular officer could call the applicant in for an interview. The applicant's essential information went into a State Department database. The information was then checked against a large "consular lookout" database called CLASS, which included a substantial watchlist of known and suspected terrorists, call TIPOFF.

Our immigration system before 9/11 focused primarily on keeping individuals intending to immigrate from improperly entering the United States. In the visa process, the most common form of fraud is to get a visa to visit the United States as a tourist and then stay to work and perhaps become a resident. Consular officers concentrated on interviewing visa applicants whom they suspected might leave and not return.

Saudi citizens rarely overstayed their visas or tried to work illegally in the United States. The same was true for citizens of the United Arab Emirates. So, while consular officials in both countries always screened applicants in CLASS, including TIPOFF, they would not interview them unless there was something about the applications that seemed problematic.

Visa applicants from these countries frequently had their applications submitted by third party facilitators, like travel agencies. In June 2001, the U.S. consular posts in Saudi Arabia instituted a third party processing program called Visa Express. It required applicants to apply through designated travel agencies instead of by mail or in person. The program was established in part to try to keep crowds of people from congregating outside the posts, which was a security risk to the posts and to the crowds themselves. We have found no evidence that the Visa Express program had any effect on the interview or approval rates for Saudi applicants, or that it reduced the scrutiny given to their applications. It actually lengthened the processing time.

With the exception of our consulates in Mexico, biometric information—like a fingerprint—was not routinely collected from visa applicants before 9/11. Terrorists therefore easily could exploit opportunities for fraud. *Khalid Sheikh Mohamed,* the chief tactical planner and coordinator of the 9/11 attacks, was indicted in 1996 by

Federal authorities in the Southern District of New York for his role in earlier terrorists plots. Yet, KSM, as he is known, obtained a visa to visit the United States on July 23, 2001, about six weeks before the 9/11 attacks. Although he is not a Saudi citizen and we do not believe he was in Saudi Arabia at the time, he applied for a visa using a Saudi passport and an alias, *Abdulrahman al Ghamdi*. He had someone else submit his application and a photo through the Visa Express program. There is no evidence that he ever used this visa to enter the United States.

Beginning in 1997, the 19 hijackers submitted 24 applications and received 23 visas. The pilots acquired most of theirs in the year 2000. The other hijackers, with two exceptions, obtained theirs between the fall of 2000 and June 2001. Two of the visas were issued in Berlin, and two were issued in the United Arab Emirates. The rest were issued in Saudi Arabia. One of the pilots, *Hani Hanjour,* had an application denied in September 2000 for lack of adequate documentation. He then produced more evidence in support of his student visa application, and it was approved. Except for *Hanjour,* all the hijackers sought tourist visas.

Of these 24 visa applications, four were destroyed routinely along with other documents before their significance was known.

To our knowledge, State consular officers followed their standard operating procedures in every case. They performed a name check using their lockout database, including the TIPOFF watchlist. At the time these people applied for visas, none of them—or at least none of the identities given in their passports—were in the database. We will say more about this in another staff statement later today.

All 20 of these applications were incomplete in some way, with a data field left blank or not answered fully. Such omissions were common. The consular officials focused on getting the biographical data needed for name checks. They generally did not think the omitted items were material to a decision about whether to issue the visa.

Three of the 19 hijackers submitted applications that contained false statements that could have been proven to be false at the time they applied. The applications of *Hani Hanjour, Saeed al Ghamdi*, and *Khalid al Mihdhar* stated that they had not previously applied for a U.S. visa when, in fact, they had. In *Hanjour's* case the false statement was made in an earlier application for a visit, in 1997, not his final visa application in 2000. *Hanjour* and *Mihdhar* also made false statements about whether they had previously traveled to the United States. Information about these prior applications was retrievable at the Jeddah post where each applied.

These false statements may have been intentional, to cover up the applicants' travel on old passports to suspect locations like Afghanistan for terrorist training. On the other hand, these statements may have been inadvertent. During this period, Saudi citizens often had their applications filled to and submitted by third parties. Most importantly, evidence of the prior visas or travel to the United States actually would have reduced concern that the applicants were intending to immigrate, so consular officers had no good reason to deny the visas or travel.

Al Mihdhar's case was uniquely problematical. He had not been entered into the TIPOFF watchlist at the time of his second visa application in June 2001. In January 2000 the American consulate in Jeddah had been asked about *Mihdhar's* visa status in conjunction with an ongoing urgent terrorist intelligence investigation and confirmed that this al Qaeda operative had a U.S. visa. When *Mihdhar* applied again in June 2001, the check against the worldwide TIPOFF watchlist took place, but no system then in place included a notation of the prior visa status check. Neither the investigating agency nor the post had made the appropriate lookout entry. Thus, in effect, the post could not 'remember' relevant suspicions a year-and-a-half earlier about his same person, who was traveling again with the same biographical information.

At least two of the hijackers were actually interviewed in person in connection with their visa applications. *Hanjour* was interviewed twice. *Satam al Suqami* was apparently interviewed in Riyadh. Another hijacker, *Ahmed al Nami,* was apparently interviewed briefly, but just to clarify an entry on his application. The three consular officers involved have some memory of these interviews. All stated that the reason for their interviews had nothing to do with terrorism. They saw nothing suspicious.

At least four individuals implicated in the 9/11 plot tried to get visas and failed: *Ramzi Binalshibh, Zakariya Essabar, Ali Abdul Aziz Ali, and Saeed al Gamdi.* This *Saeed al Gamdi* is a different person from the *Saeed al Ghamdi* who actually became a hijacker.

Ramzi Binalshibh, a Yemeni, apparently intended to train as a pilot along with his Hamburg friends, *Mohamed Atta, Marwan al Shehhi,* and *Ziad Jarrah. Binalshibh* applied for a visa three times in Berlin and once in Yemen. He first applied in Berlin on the same day as Atta. He was interviewed twice and denied twice. Yemen is a much poorer country than Saudi Arabia. Both times, consular officers determined he did not have strong ties to Germany and he might be intending to immigrate unlawfully to the United States. *Binalshibh* tried again in Berlin, this time for a student visa to attend aviation school in Florida. He was denied again for lack of adequate documentation and failure to show sufficient ties to Germany.

Essabar, a Moroccan who may also have intended to be a pilot, tried to get a visa in Berlin at least once and failed because he failed to demonstrate sufficient ties to Germany, such as a job or family there. Third country visa applicants in Berlin were held to significantly higher standards—in terms of documentation and showing ties with their country of residence—than were Saudi and Emirati citizens applying from their own countries.

Ali Abdul Aziz is the nephew of Khalid Sheikh Mohamed and was heavily involved in financial and logistical aspects of the 9/11 plot. He tried to get a U.S. visa in Dubai about two weeks before the attacks. His visa application states that he intended to enter the United States on September 4, 2001, for one week. As a Pakistani visa applicant in a third country, he would have received greater scrutiny from U.S. officials from the start. In any event, it was deemed possible that he intended to immigrate, and accordingly he was denied a visa.

Saeed al Gamdi, also know as "Jihad" al Gamdi, apparently intended to participate in the 9/11 attacks. He is a Saudi and applied for a tourist visa in Jeddah on November 12, 2000, the same date as 9/11 hijacker *Ahmad al Haznawi. Haznawi* was approved, but *al Gamdi* was denied after an interview with a consular officer, because the consular officer believed he was intending to immigrate.

Entry into and exit from the United States

With a visa, an individual can travel to a United States port of entry. Upon arrival, the individual must seek admission into the United States from an inspector of what used to be called the INS, an agency whose personnel now form part of the Department of Homeland Security. Property being brought into the United States is checked by inspectors of the U.S. Customs Service, whose personnel are now also part of the DHA.

The 19 hijackers entered the United States a total of 33 times. They arrived through ten different airports, though more than half came in from Miami, JFK, or Newark. A visitor with a tourist visa was usually admitted for a stay of six months. All but two of the hijackers were admitted for such stays. *Hanjour* had a student visa and was admitted for a stay of two years, and *Suqami* sought and was admitted for a stay of 20 days.

The four pilots passed through INS and Customs inspections a total of 17 times before 9/11. *Hanjour* came to the United States to attend school in three stints during the 1990s. His final arrival was in December 2000, through the Cincinnati/Northern Kentucky airport.

The other three pilots, *Atta, al Shehhi,* and *Jarrah,* initially came in May and June 2000. They arrived for the last time between May and August 2001. All made a number of trips aboard during their extended stays in the United States.

Of the other 15, only *Mihdhar* entered the United States, left, and returned. *Nawaf al Hazmi* arrived in January 2000 with *Mihdhar* and stayed. *Al Mihdhar* left in June 2000 and returned to the United States on July 4, 2001. Ten of the others came in pairs between April and June 2001. Three more arrived through Miami on May 28.

The INS inspector usually had about one to one and a half minutes to assess the traveler and make a decision on admissibility and length of stay. For all the entries, a primary INS inspector would work a lane of incoming travelers and check the people and their passports. The inspector would try to assess each individual's demeanor. No one noted any anomalies in these passports despite the fact, we now believe, that at least two and as many as eight showed evidence of fraudulent manipulation. The inspector would use the passport data, especially if it was machine readable to check various INS and Customs databases. The databases would show the person's immigration history information, as well as terrorist watchlist and criminal history information.

Of the five hijackers who entered the United States more than once, three of them violated immigration law.

Ziad Jarrah entered in June 2000 on a tourist visa and then promptly enrolled in flight school for six months. He never filed an application to change his immigration status from tourist to student. Had the INS known he was out of status, they could have denied him entry on any of the three subsequent occasions he departed and returned while he was a student.

Marwan al Shehhi came in through Newark in late May 2000, followed a week later by *Mohamed Atta.* Both were admitted as tourists and soon entered flight school in Florida. In September they did file applications to change their status. Before 9/11, regulations allowed tourists to change their status at any time, so they were in compliance. But both overstayed their periods of admission and completed flight school to obtain commercial pilot licenses. *Atta* and *al Shehhi* then left within a few days of one another and returned within a few days of one another in January 2001, while their change in visa status from tourist to student was still pending.

Atta and *al Shehhi* did get some attention when both said they were coming back to finish flight school. Primary inspectors noticed with each that their story clashed with their attempt to reenter on tourist visas. The rules required them to get proper student visas while they had been overseas, since their earlier pending applications for a change of status were considered abandoned once they left the United States. *Atta* and *al Shehhi* were each referred by the primary inspectors to secondary inspection.

At secondary, more experienced inspectors could conduct long interviews, check more databases, take fingerprints, examine personal property, and call on other agencies for help. The inspectors involved have stated they do not remember these encounters. The reports indicate that both men repeated their story about still going to flight school and their pending applications for a change of status. The secondary inspectors admitted *Atta* and *al Shehhi* as tourists.

Flight 93 hijacker *Saeed al Ghamdi* was referred to secondary immigration inspection when he arrived in late June 2001. He had no address on him I-94 form. He spoke little English. He had a one-way ticket and about $500. The inspector wondered whether he was possibly intending to immigrate. *Al Ghamdi* convinced the inspector that he was a tourist and had enough money.

Customs officers took a second look at two of the hijackers but then admitted them. On *Marwan al Shehhi's* first entry into the United States, a customs officer referred him to secondary inspection, completed the inspection, and released him. In May 2001, *Waleed al*

Shehri and *Satam Suqami* departed Florida for the Bahamas but were refused admission. On their way back to the United States, a customs officer conducting a pre-clearance in the Bahamas referred *al Shehri* to a second inspection. Customs then released *al Shehri* to return to the United States with *Suqami.*

We do know of one success by immigration secondary inspection that affected the 9/11 plot. An al Qaedo operative, *Mohamed al Kahtani,* arrived at Orlando airport on August 4, 2001. Evidence strongly suggests that *Mohamed Atta* was waiting there to meet him. *Kahtani* encountered an experienced and dedicated inspector, Jose Melendez-Perez. We will hear his story later this morning.

During their stays in the United States at least six of the 9/11 hijackers violated immigration laws. We have noted *Jarrah's* failure to adjust his status while he was in flight school and the violations by *Atta* and *al Shehhi. Hani Hanjour* came on a student visa in December 2000 but then did not attend the English language school for which his visa was issued. *Nawaf al Hazmi* overstayed his term of admission by nine months. *Suqami* overstayed his term of admission by four months. None of these violations were detected or acted upon by INS inspectors or agents.

Two programs might have helped detect such violations. One dealt with violations of student status. The other dealt with overstays.

National security concerns about foreign students are not new. By the late 1980s the INS had established a Student/School System to track students, but the system did not work. After the 1993 World Trade Center bombing, when it was discovered that a participant in the plot had been a student who had overstayed his visa, the Department of Justice asked INS to devise a better way to track students. INS officials recommended a new student tracking system and a student ID card that used biometric identifiers.

In 1996, Congress mandated a new system to be installed by 1998, without appropriating program funds. The INS scraped together $10 million and piloted a successful student tracking program in the Atlanta area in June 1997, which included a flight school. However, advocates of education interests argued that the program would be burdensome and costly. Upon the order of senior INS management, the project manager was replaced. In 1998, INS indefinitely deferred testing of the biometric student ID card. The program stalled. Senators declared an interest in repealing the 1996 law and sought to obstruct further INS funding for it. Thus, when *Atta* and *al Shehhi* lied when questioned about their student status on their reentries in January 2001, and when *Hanjour* failed to show up for the school for which he was issued a visa in December 2000, a student tracking system was far from available to immigration inspectors or agents.

Congress required the Attorney General to develop an entry-exit system in 1996. The system's purpose was to improve INS's ability to address illegal migration and overstays of all types of foreign visitors. By 1998, Congress had appropriated about $40 million to develop the system. Advocates for border communities, however, were concerned that an entry-exit system would slow down trade. INS officials decided to forego the system at the land borders and only to automate the entry process. The automation process was not successful. The result was that when hijackers *Suqami* and *Nawaf al Hazmi* overstayed their visas, the system Congress envisaged did not exist. Moreover, when federal law enforcement authorities realized in late August 2001 that *Mihdhar* had entered with *Hazmi* in January 2000 at Lost Angeles, they could not reliably determine whether or not *Hazmi* was still in the United States, along with *Mihdhar*.

Conclusion

The Director of the FBI testified that "[e]ach of the hijackers… came easily and lawfully from abroad." The Director of Central Intelligence described 17 of the 19 hijackers as "clean." We believe the information we have provided today gives the Commission the opportunity to reevaluate those statements. Based on our evaluation of the hijackers' travel documents, the visa process, the entries into the United States, and the compliance with immigration law while the attackers were here, we have a few observations. Considered collectively, the 9/11 hijackers:

- Included among them know al Qaeda operatives who could have been watchlisted;
- Presented passports "manipulated in a fraudulent manner;"
- Presented passports with "suspicious indicators" of extremism;
- Made detectable false statements on their visa applications;
- Were pulled out of the travel stream and given greater scrutiny by border officials;
- Made false statements to border officials to gain entry to the United States; and
- Violated immigration laws while inside the United States.

These circumstances offered opportunities to intelligence and law enforcement officials. But our government did not fully exploit al Qaeda's travel vulnerabilities.

Why weren't they exploited? We do not have all the answers. Certainly neither the State Department's consular officers nor the INS's inspectors and agents were ever considered full partners in a national counterterrorism effort. This is exemplified by the Bureau of Consular Affairs' statement that before 9/11 they were not informed by anyone in the State Department or elsewhere that Saudi citizens could pose security risks. Nor were the Consular Affairs bureau or INS given the resources to perform an expanded mission. Between 1998 and 2001, visa applications rose nearly a third, an increase of 2.5 million per year. Trained staff did not keep pace with the volume increase. In Jeddah and Riyadh, for example, each consular officer had responsibility for processing, on average, about 30,000 applications per year and routinely interviewed about 200 people per day.

The INS before 9/11 had about 2,000 agents for interior enforcement. As long as the top enforcement priorities were removal of criminal aliens and prosecution of employers who hired illegal aliens, a major counterterrorism effort would not have been possible. This is not to pass judgment on immigration policy generally. What we can do is highlight the way those policy choices affected counterterrorism efforts before 9/11, and potentially affect them today. For our front line border inspection services to have taken a substantially more proactive role in counterterrorism, their missions would have had to have been considered integral to our national security strategy and given commensurate resources.

Today, the level of systematic effort by the intelligence community focused on terrorist travel is much greater. But terrorist travel intelligence is still seen as a niche effort, interesting for specialists, but not central to counterterrorism. Nor have policymakers fully absorbed the information developed by terrorist mobility specialists. Much remains to be done, within the United States and internationally, on travel and identity document security, penalties and enforcement policy with respect to document fraud, and travel document screening efforts at the borders. If we have one conclusion from our work so far, it is that disrupting terrorist mobility globally is at least as important as disrupting terrorist finance as an integral part of counterterrorism.

APPENDIX TO
STAFF STATEMENT NO. 1

9/11 HIJACKERS AND CONSPIRATORS

American Airlines Flight 11

Mohamed Atta	Hijacker (Pilot)
Abdul Aziz al Omari	Hijacker
Waleed al Shehri	Hijacker
Satam al Suqami	Hijacker
Wail al Shehri	Hijacker

American Airlines Flight 77

Hani Hanjour	Hijacker (Pilot)
Khalid al Mihdhar	Hijacker
Majed Moqed	Hijacker
Nawaf al Hazmi	Hijacker
Salem al Hazmi	Hijacker

United Airlines Flight 93

Ziad Samir Jarrah	Hijacker (Pilot)
Saeed al Ghamdi	Hijacker
Ahmed al Nami	Hijacker
Ahmed al Haznawi	Hijacker

United Airlines Flight 175

Marwan al Shehhi   Hijacker (Pilot)
Mohand al Shehri   Hijacker
Hamza al Ghamdi   Hijacker
Fayez Banihammad   Hijacker
Ahmed al Ghamdi   Hijacker

Other Conspirators

Khalid Sheikh Mohamed   Mastermind
Ramzi Binalshibh   Potential Pilot
Zakariya Essabar   Potential Pilot/Hijacker
Saeed "Jihad" al Gamdi   Potential Hijacker
Ali Abdul Aziz Ali   Financial Facilitator
Mohamed al Kahtani   Potential Hijacker

Airline Passenger Screening Has Become a
FEMA-TYPE SNAFU

The Screening System Developed During 1969-70 Holds The Key To Refocusing On Modern Day Terrorism

PROLOGUE

This updated sequel is a revision and expansion of my previous book on airline passenger screening titled, *NINE/ELEVEN*. In some instances, I have used literary license.

Airline passenger screening by the Transportation Security Administration (TSA) in particular, and Mideast terrorism in general, have elements in common. The government should relearn the basic meticulous approaches and conclusions from the original screening program.

I also submit that Mideast terrorists have outsmarted us by switching targets and tactics.

The following observations are based on my unique professional experience:

(1) Mideast terrorists have easier targets of opportunity in the U.S. with lower risk than to repeat the kamikaze-type attacks of 9/11/2001.

(2) Mideast terrorists are winning the psychological war. Just a rumor of an intended incident spreads fear in this country. And, their audience is as much Islam as U.S.

(3) Mideast terrorists have succeeded in diverting billions of U.S. dollars from our domestic needs. How long can we balance both requirements?

(4) The government continues to treat the symptoms of Mideast terrorism, not address the root causes.

CHAPTER ONE —
IF IT'S BROKE, FIX IT

Panic has given birth to the fraternal twins Department of Homeland Security and Transportation Security Administration. Their godfathers are Department of Transportation and Federal Aviation Administration, relatively speaking.

There is a saying on The National Archives wall in downtown Washington, D.C. copied from Shakespeare's "The Tempest." It reads: "The Past is Prologue." George Santayana, in his "The Life of Reason," wrote: "Those who cannot remember the past are condemned to repeat it."

And, that is exactly how to describe the Rube Goldberg approach to airport passenger screening that is in vogue today, and its relationship to Mideast terrorism.

The current screening system is not as efficient nor effective as it could be because it is based on a set of faulty premises and assumptions. The past needs to be re-examined for sensible repairs. Instead, decision makers are acting like hamsters, running fast in place and getting nowhere. On July 12, 2005, the Secretary of the Department of Homeland Security announced yet another "reorganization."

With the fifth anniversary of 9/11 coming up in 2006, just what has been accomplished? Mideast terrorists, and their disciples, keep changing their *modus operandi,* but we have not. We seem bent on remodeling the Edsel instead of redesigning a new vehicle to fight terrorism.

We seem to be trying to combat terrorism in the 21st century with 20th century tactics. For the first time, this country is fighting religious-based scattered guerillas, not an organized government-based. army. The demolition of organized Iraqi military forces was textbook tactics. But, instead of the end of the book, we find more and more unexpected chapters. We literally need a new beginning, and experience from the original airline passenger screening effort will help.

CHAPTER TWO —
THE INTERVIEW BEGINS

SM: "Mr. Brown, I am a staff member of the National Commission on Terrorist Attacks Upon the United States, most often called the 9/11 Commission. I am telephoning you because it has come to our attention that you have written a book on airport security based on a Federal Aviation Administration Task Force that only was in effect for a year and a half."

DB: "Actually, I already have written one titled *NINE/ELEVEN*. I am working on a sequel titled, *MIDEAST TERRORISTS MAY NOT BOTHER WITH ANOTHER 9/11.*

SM: "That's very provocative. Can you come in for an interview?"

DB: "I would be happy to do so. Dr. John T. Dailey, my colleague, is a frail 89 years old, but I have his background material."

SM: "Thank you for coming. Where should we start?"

DB: "I would like to begin with what passes for airline passenger screening today, and why I feel it is not accomplishing the task for which it was developed more than three decades ago. Our Final Report, issued in 1978 as FAA Manual AM-78-35, described pre-Task Force efforts as a poorly coordinated rush toward prevention with assorted, often contradictory, determinations regarding useful means of control. How does that sound when compared to today's efforts?"

SM: "What do you mean by that?"

DB: "I brought along my first book because it is the only one that contains the behind-the-scenes look at how screening was first developed by that Task Force during 1969-70. Airlines knew our conclusions. One of those conclusions ironically predicted that 'mass hijacking of U.S. aircraft could also be carried out by an organized group in order to achieve terrorist objectives.'"

SM: "Are you implying the Task Force predicted 9/11 ?"

DB: "In a way, yes. But, we did not envision those hijacked aircraft would be used as flying missiles. However, all of the nine members of the team were well aware of how the Japanese used suicide attacks against our naval forces in the Pacific during World War II."

SM: "Then, what are you implying?"

DB: "I need to go back in time to the origin of the Task Force, and what our goal was before I connect it with the present. There are those who wonder why the effort was turned over to the Office of Aviation Medicine. The Final Report explained that the Task Force needed to be made up of specialists from many disciplines 'to explore all facets of (skyjacking) in a simultaneous, coordinated and systematic manner.' The field of medicine utilizes an approach called epidemiology which looks into the 'nature of a disease, to substantiate a conclusion statistically, to pinpoint locations of an outbreak and to define within reasonable levels of accuracy the elements of the outbreak and the probabilities for its continued spread.' Thus, this approach points up the similarities to be found in effective efforts to track down elusive disease-causing entities and control of the kinds of circumstances involved in air piracy - assuming, of course, that epidemiological methodology is appropriately modified and applied to (air piracy).'"

SM: "That is a mouthful and a half, but I think I understand this approach."

DB: "That set the tone for our group, chaired by Dr. H.L. (Rick) Reighard, the FAA's federal air surgeon. Our top priority clearly was to develop and test a system that could help stem the tide of aircraft hijackings, most of which went to Cuba. But, by the very title of the group, we knew early on that there never could be one system that could *eliminate* all hijackings."

SM: "So, what was your goal?"

DB: "Our goal was to try to reduce hijacking *attempts* to a manageable number. The odds of dealing with such problems are infinitely better on the ground than in the air."

SM: "How did you hope to do that?"

DB: "We did not have the luxury of any precedents to guide us. But, the luck of timing stepped in. Dr. Dailey had been working on creating psychological profiles for years. By the time he joined the FAA as chief psychologist in early 1968, he had developed and applied dozens of profile tests to several million Air Force and Navy personnel, as well as to students at Texas, Pittsburgh, and George Washington Universities. On February 6, 1969, Congressman Harley 0. Staggers chaired a hearing of his House Committee on Interstate and Foreign Commerce. Dr. Dailey's closed-door plea to test his new behavioral profile as Step One of a passenger screening system turned out to be the key for a Committee mandate ordering the FAA to create the Task Force."

SM: "I heard somewhere that the Task Force was disbanded after only a year and a half. Does that mean you accomplished your goal in such a short time?"

CHAPTER THREE —
VITAL MISTAKES

D B: "Yes, but disbanding our Task Force was one of two horrific mistakes that changed the course of history. However, to respond to your statement, Dr. Reighard said from the beginning that he hoped our work would lead to the establishment of a permanent office within the FAA. He lobbied to have Task Force members form the nucleus of a permanent entity. Pages 76-80 of the Final Report contain recommendations for the staffing. But, when the Office of Air Transportation Security was created shortly after we were disbanded in August 1970, only our security representative joined it full time. Another member became sort of a consultant."

SM: "Why was that a mistake? Sounds more like bureaucratic sour grapes."

DB: "That broke the link between what we accomplished and what was implemented later on. The new Office personnel literally had to reinvent the wheel. We did the testing. On the one hand, the passengers we interviewed did not have any objections to some sort of search. I was on the testing team that went to all nine airports, and I videotaped passenger reaction. More important, Dr. Dailey concluded from the data the other members of the testing team garnered that no more than **2 percent** of the flying public fit enough of his profile to be subjected to a further and more intensive search and interrogation. We wanted a procedure that had verified merit, and that focused on the most **likely** potential hijackers. In doing so, we could facilitate screening out the other 98 percent of passengers. In my previous book, I pointed out that airlines warned that we would ruin air travel by *overly intrusive* searching. But, if we could quickly and efficiently clear those 98 percent, detaining the 2 percent would be manageable and tolerable."

SM: "Even with all the searching going on today, air travel is not suffering."

DB: "No, but the current procedure has not caught any Mideast terrorists. And, results are highly suspect, if you will forgive the pun. Look at what we have today. The media keep reporting cases of searches that humiliate many older and many younger passengers, of equipment that breaks down, of security personnel who are not doing a professional job, et cetera, et cetera, et cetera. On May 8, 2005, The New York Times had this headline: 'U.S. to Spend Billions More to Alter Security Systems.'"

SM: "You said there were two mistakes. What was the other one?"

DB: "That took place during what has been labeled 'Black September of 1970.' Following a sort of truce between Israel and Egypt, several radical organizations broke away from the Palestine Liberation Organization, or PLO. One, the Popular Front for the Liberation of Palestine, or PFLP, decided to hijack four airplanes to gain the release of fellow guerillas whom the Israelis had captured and who were sent to Swiss jails. On September 6, a Nicaraguan man and a Palestinian woman hijacked El Al Flight 219 that had taken off from Tel Aviv headed for New York's JFK Airport. El Al guards aboard the flight killed the man and captured the woman, Leila Khaled. The plane flew on to London's Heathrow Airport. On that same day, two hijackers, who were supposed to be on the El Al flight but who were bumped off because the plane was full, hijacked Pan Am Flight 93 after it left Brussels also headed for JFK. They flew to Beirut to refuel, and several other hijackers got aboard. The plane finally landed in Cairo, Egypt. After all passengers and crew left the plane, the hijackers blew it up. TWA Flight 74 was hijacked after it left Frankfurt Germany, and was flown to a former British Royal Air Force base in Jordan called Dawson's Field. Swissair Flight 100 was hijacked after leaving Zurich, and also taken there."

SM: "That was some feat."

DB: "That wasn't all. Three days later, a lone hijacker took over BOAC Flight 775 and brought it to Dawson's Field. It turned out the hijacker was not a member of the PFLP, but a Palestinian sympathetic to the cause who wanted Khaled freed."

SM: "What happened then?"

DB: 'The hijackers cut a deal for the release of Khaled, after which they blew up the three planes at Dawson's Field."

SM: "You said 'Black September' was a mistake."

DB: "Shortly afterward, the Nixon administration ordered that all passengers boarding U.S. planes were to be searched."

SM: "So, what's wrong with that?"

DB: "What's wrong is that *not one* of those aircraft was hijacked in the United States. Why order the screening of all passengers in *our* country when the hijackings took place in *other* countries?"

SM: "I repeat, what's wrong with that?"

DB: "Actually, that very good question leads directly into formation of our Task Force. Other countries around the world have their own systems of screening passengers. We only developed and tested a viable procedure for screening passengers in the United States. While we looked at how other countries dealt with hijackers, we focused on what was feasible in our nation. We concluded that what works in one country does not necessarily work in other countries."

SM: "Let's back up a bit to where the Task Force came into being."

CHAPTER FOUR —
BIRTH OF A CREATION

DB: "Little more than a week after the Staggers Committee mandate, FAA Acting Administrator Dave Thomas tepidly created the Task Force on Deterrence of Air Piracy. The term 'deterrence' is very important."

SM: "Why is that?"

DB: "Because, we agreed that there was no way we could eliminate all hijackings. Our goal was to get the odds in our favor by developing a procedure targeted for a manageable number of what we called 'suspects.' We felt from the beginning that trying to screen every airline passenger would be inefficient, ineffective, and disruptive."

SM: "But, aren't all passengers screened today? Are you implying that the current procedures are, to use your own words, inefficient, ineffective, and disruptive?"

DB: "For the most part, yes. But there are some good elements to the current system."

SM: "All right, continue with the Task Force time line."

DB: "Except for Dr. Reighard and Dr. Dailey, who as chief psychologist was on his staff, none of the team members knew each other. We came from diverse disciplines: Lowell L. Davis from Flight Standards Service; Joseph K. Blank from Office of Compliance and Security; Max Collins from Aircraft Development; John E. Marsh from Office of General Counsel; Robert K. Friedman from Office of Management Systems; E. Lee Jett from Office of International Aviation

Affairs, and me from Office of Public Affairs. Thus, we had input from specialists in security, operations, engineering, law, management, international aviation, behavioral sciences and medicine, and media relations. By the end of our work, as diverse professionally as we were, we had become friends and even socialized together."

SM: "Isn't that unusual for government workers?"

DB: "Yes. But, I like to feel we were the right persons together at the right time for the right purpose. That is not to say it started out that way. I only can speak for myself. As the press officer, I was treated with cool hostility. I had the distinct feeling the others felt that I would blab everything to the news media. Some of our work had to be secret. I actually had to be 'tested' by some of the group."

SM: "Go on."

DB: "Dr. Reighard seemed the wrong choice to be chairman. He was basically a very shy person. He told me once that he was not even comfortable holding a staff meeting with his own people. As a physician, he had a keen sense of diagnosing problems before prescribing remedies. In hindsight, I only now realize that his medical approach to hijacking was so right on target. *Because of that, I firmly believe Mideast terrorism is a cancer on society. If not treated properly, it will become more virulent and spread.* Getting back to Dr. Reighard, he listened to everyone, and encouraged all of us to exchange views and information. As a result, we effectively worked 'outside of the box.' We wanted results, and were willing to take chances with new approaches to what we found in our testing phase. We did not want to be tied down by bureaucratic red tape. We had to find a way to deter potential hijackers from boarding their flights in the first place. *Ironically, that is the same Number One priority today!*"

SM: "Well, if the Number One priority has not changed, why are you so critical of what is going on today?"

DB: "When we did our work, hijackers were not Mideast terrorists.

They were for the most part ordinary citizens who wanted to hijack aircraft, but not to kill passengers or themselves. The 9/11 hijackers were suicide terrorists who wanted to kill both themselves and all the other passengers to make their political statement."

CHAPTER FIVE —
THE PROPER FOCUS

SM: "That's an interesting distinction."

DB: "Dr. Dailey's behavioral profile was focused on screening out *potential* hijackers while facilitating the boarding of the other 98 percent of the passengers. So, the basic premise was that passengers were *innocent* until the profile, plus subsequent search and interrogation, proved otherwise. Today, all passengers are presumed to be potential Mideast terrorists until they can prove their innocense."

SM: "And, your point is?"

DB: "My point is that if all your security efforts are aimed at requiring 100 percent of the passengers to prove they are not potential Mideast terrorists, you just cannot have an efficient, effective, and non-humiliating search procedure. I say again, our goal was to efficiently and quickly facilitate the boarding of those 98 percent of passengers while focusing with those 2 percent suspects. The government should go back to Square One to determine how to identify potential Mideast terrorists. I emphasize *potential Mideast terrorists,* not Americans. Let me give you a personal example of how questionable the current system is."

SM: "This should be interesting."

DB: "Last year, my wife and I went on a tour of European countries. On our return, we had to change planes in Philadelphia for our flight back to Dulles International Airport. Of the 39 passengers, I was the only one selected for a personal search."

SM: "Why?"

DB: "I asked the same question. Believe it or not, the answer was, 'We have to search at least one person on every flight.'"

SM: "And, what was your response to this? Did you tell him you were on the team that developed passenger screening in the beginning?"

DB: "I tried a different tack. I offered my passport and my round-trip airline tickets. I tried to reason that a potential Mideast terrorist would not likely take his wife on a two-week European vacation before returning to the U.S. to do a dirty deed. One of the elements in our original profile was that hijackers would buy one-way tickets, not round-trip ones. 'Why spend the extra money when you are not going to be alive for the return flight?' I asked. He did not think that was funny. By the way, no one searched my wife."

SM: "If I understand what you are saying, it is that passengers with valid identification should not be searched the same way potential hijackers are. But, documents can be forged. That happened on 9/11."

DB: "There is a world of difference between searching for *potential Mideast terrorist hijackers* and searching for *potential non-Mideast terrorist hijackers.* By the way, I am a retired Army Reserve lieutenant colonel. I carry that photo-ID in my wallet. But, I will bet that still would not have satisfied that security guard.*"

SM: "Wait a minute. Didn't the 19 terrorists - I mean Mideast terrorists - have identification that passed security?"

DB: "Yes. And, that makes another point. Dr. Dailey's behavioral profile had some two dozen characteristics. Just one would not be cause for concern. If memory serves me correctly, at least half a dozen would be a minimum to label a passenger as a 'suspect.'"

SM: "What about the name-watch list that the FBI and CIA have developed?"

DB: "That's after-the-fact. Since there has been so much publicity about a name list, what terrorist in his right mind would continue to use a name that was likely to be on that list?"

SM: "I recall that in early July of 2005, a passenger was hauled off a flight because his name was on the name-watch list."

DB: "I am not denying that the name-watch list could have some value. In fact, there are numerous stories about planes that have made emergency landings, because after the flight was airborne authorities discovered a name on the list. Those stories also have pointed out that many innocent Mideast people have the same name. In 1976, way before all the terrorism took hold, I was stopped at JFK International Airport on a return trip from Israel, taken aside, and questioned. It seemed a New York City criminal with the same first, middle initial, and last name as mine was on the FBI's Most Wanted List. It took me several minutes to assure the officer that I never had resided in New York City."

SM: "Better safe than sorry, wouldn't you say?"

DB: "I would agree, only if you add sensible safe than sorry."

SM: " What's wrong with that? I remember that passenger who had an explosive device hidden in his shoe."

DB: "You are referring to the so-called 'shoe bomber.' He was a domestic nut case who professed a love for Mideast terrorism. As far as I can tell, *no terrorist hijacker born in the Middle East* has been found with such a device in his shoe on a U.S. airplane. Remember I pointed out that we could not eliminate all hijacking attempts. We readily admitted some attempts could breach any security system. As tight as security is in the Mideast, there still have been attempted terrorist activities while the aircraft was in flight."

SM: "So, are you saying the government should not check for another potential 'shoe bomber?"

DB: "No. I am saying you have to identify what you are searching for, using a combination of the profile and technology. But, with proper ID, get the innocent passengers on board their flights.

SM: "Wow! I am confused."

DB: "What I am saying is that once the 'shoe bomber' incident was over, the metal detector screening system should have been adjusted to check for such a device. Merely triggering the magnetometer should not require a full body search if the passenger has proper ID, or can meet other clearance criteria."

SM: "Are you saying the detectors can be flexible?"

DB: "Each airline can adjust the detectors at various airports. Dr. Dailey always maintained that his behavioral profile was flexible enough to be adjusted depending on the type of hijackings taking place. A May 3, 2005 story in The New York Times noted that a female FBI agent was allowed to pass through security with her pistol, but her nail file was confiscated as a potential weapon."

SM: "We seem to be getting deeper and deeper into this, and I apologize for having to take another break. I have another commitment this afternoon. I wonder if you could return the day after tomorrow."

DB: "Absolutely."

CHAPTER SIX —
THE PRE-BOARDING PROFILE

SM: "Let"s start off today with what steps can keep the hijackers from boarding."

DB: "We need to understand the behavioral approach. Citing the Final Report, this approach 'is statistical in character and involves analysis of such factors as: (1) What kinds of persons engage in a particular activity? (2) How do they go about it? (3) Why do they do it?"

SM: " Why is this important?"

DB: "Again, we turn to the Final Report: 'Examination of statistical probabilities tends to reveal when and under what circumstances the unwanted activity may take place.' The difference between what we did then, and what is going on now, is that there are no 'statistical probabilities' in current procedures. The government merely decided to screen everyone, as if that simple procedure would address the complex problem. And, that is why Dr. Dailey's profile gained so much credibility."

SM: "If I understand what you are saying, this methodical approach is what led to what you call success."

DB: "Yes, and I am glad you used the term 'success.' Let me put it another way. In 1961, Congress passed the Air Piracy Act. That made it a crime to try to hijack an airplane. I submit that is all well and fine for rational people like you and me. It certainly does not address terrorists, who are irrational by our definition. We must keep in mind that the 9/11 terrorist hijackers could not care less about the Air Piracy Act. They were going to die, and so were all the passengers. And, again keep in mind, our work was not concerned with Mideast terrorist hijackers. All I am saying is that before the current procedures were rushed into action, they should have been subjected to the same methodological approach we used."

SM: "All right, let's get back to the purpose of the profile once it was proposed."

DB: "I must reiterate that we never hoped to keep all **potential** hijackers from boarding. We wanted to deal with a manageable number."

SM: "I will try to remember that. How did you hope to accomplish that goal?"

DB: "That is where Dr. Dailey proved so invaluable. Using his previous profiling experience with the FAA's own two-stage screening program for civilian pilots, John conducted an exhaustive research of all previous hijackings - successful or not - to create the most complete data bank on the subject in existence. He and I also produced the first complete list of hijackings, which were used not only by the International Civil Aviation Organization, as well as by many countries throughout the world, and also by the various news media."

SM: "What did Dr. Dailey's research conclude?"

DB: "He discovered that a number of characteristics seemed to discriminate innocent passengers from past hijackers who posed as innocent passengers. He refined that list down to about two dozen characteristics that would avoid being labeled 'racial profiling.' Let me cite public data from Pages 58-59 of the Final Report: 'After evaluating what was learned during testing, Task Force members placed emphasis on accumulating data on the age and sex of passengers; place, time, and payment of tickets; boarding sequence; pre-boarding activity; time of day, origin of flight, type of aircraft, destination, duration of flight, segment traveled, and geographic direction of flight; whether the passenger traveled alone or was with someone; whether the passenger had carry-on luggage and had luggage checked in the boarding sequence; and, seat selection.' A one-way ticket was an obvious clue."

SM: "You've got to be kidding me. Those are just common sense."

DB: "Sometimes the obvious escapes you. But, John was meticulous. Anyhow, that became Step One in our proposed procedure.'

SM: "For the sake of argument, let's say someone triggered enough of that profile to make them suspect. What then?"

DB: "Step Two would require that person to produce valid identification. Step Three would require that person to pass through a metal detector called a magnetometer. That is the same off-the-shelf device soldiers used in World War II to locate land mines. It's the same device people use on beaches to find discarded worthwhile metal objects."

SM: "And, then?"

DB: "Step Four would involve a body scan by a hand-held version of the magnetometer, followed by extensive interrogation."

SM: "Do I infer from what you have described that it is important to conduct those steps in the order you have listed?"

DB: "Absolutely! We concluded that upsetting that procedure would render the system ineffective. In fact, that issue came up in a court case I will discuss later."

SM: "Now that you had this procedure, what did you do next?"

DB: "We needed to test John's profile."

SM:"Why?"

DB: "First, we needed to find out if it provided a viable approach. Second, we needed to know how many passengers fit enough of that profile to be set aside."

CHAPTER SEVEN —
TESTING, TESTING – STEP ONE

SM: "How were you going to conduct the testing?"

DB: "At first, the group wanted to try it out only at New York's LaGuardia Airport and Miami's International Airport. Those seemed to be the favorite boarding places. Then, someone wanted to include Washington's National Airport."

SM: "Sounds reasonable."

DB: "I was the newest and youngest member of the Task Force, but my gut feeling was that we needed more testing sites. Early in my newspaper career, I had done some market research, and it taught me to get enough inclusion in the research so that the results would not get skewed."

SM: "Screwed?"

DB: "No, s-k-e-w-e-d. I did not want the results to be distorted."

SM: "How did the others react?"

DB: "Bless Dr. Reighard, he agreed immediately. He relied on his medical background to get as much unbiased data as possible before reaching a conclusion. We finally agreed on five other airports around the country, and the airport in San Juan, Puerto Rico."

SM: "What was your reasoning?"

DB: "I felt passengers flew in and out of different parts of the country for different reasons."

SM: "How did the others react to that?"

DB: "Well, not as bad as they did to my next suggestion."

SM: "And, what was that one?"

DB: "To be honest, I sucked in my breath, and then recommended that we hold press conferences at every one of the airports. I got some angry stares, believe me. But first, I have to explain how we were going to conduct the tests, and how the press conference would fit in."

SM: "Go ahead."

DB: 'Dr. Reighard determined that the testing team would consist of Lowell Davis, Max Collins, and me. Lowell had been a Navy pilot; Max had been a civilian one. Our work would be only with Eastern Air Lines at its gates at each one of the airports."

SM: "Why Eastern?"

DB: "At the time, it was the most hijacked airline."

SM: "Sounds reasonable."

DB: "There would be two parts to the testing. As I pointed out before, one was to determine what percentage of Eastern's passengers fit enough of the profile to be labeled a 'suspect.' The second was for me to use a videotape recorder to document passenger reaction. Actually, there really was a third, now that I think of it. Since I got the go-ahead to hold press conferences, that would give us a clue to media reaction."

SM: "What was your routine?'

DB: "First, we visited the designated airport. We checked out the test gate, and Lowell and Max briefed gate personnel. Then, about two weeks later, we flew back to set up the magnetometer and my videotape recorder. Also, I had alerted the news media in that city that a press conference would be held to test a passenger screening system designed to discourage potential hijackers. Thanks to Lowell and Max, the testing went smoothly. As passengers passed through our portable magnetometer, Eastern personnel would ask passengers at random how they felt about being screened, while I videotaped their comments. Meanwhile, Lowell and Max would monitor Eastern gate personnel who had been briefed on the profile to keep track of how many passengers triggered it."

SM: "What about the reporters?"

DB: "We did our homework back in Dr. Reighard's office. My reasoning, based on nearly 15 years as an Ohio newspaper reporter before I became a government public information officer, was that the media would soon learn about the screening, and smell a story on why it was secret. I argued that if we told the media in advance about the magnetometer, we could nip in the bud any stories about how reporters 'beat a secret system.' In fact, we invited the reporters to go through the detector. I also tried to anticipate questions the reporters would ask, and the rest of the team helped me formulate the proper answers."

SM: "What if the reporters asked questions about the profile?"

DB: "Thanks to the team, we worked out our response. All I would say was that we were developing a procedure that could identify potential hijackers that included electronic search. I would add that I could not reveal further details because of security concerns."

SM: "How did that work out?"

DB: "Of course, reporters wanted to know all about that profile. When I would not give specifics, they usually pressed me hard for details. Oh, sorry for that pun."

SM: "How did you handle that?"

DB: "The response probably would not work today, what with such a determined news media. I would say that if I revealed the details, any potential hijacker would know how to beat the profile. I would ask, 'If you revealed the profile, would you want a member of your family, or even yourself, to be on the next flight out?' As expected, there were those few reporters who scoffed at the testing. What helped was that, with the team's agreement, I would announce that this was an experimental system that was not foolproof, but was an approach we felt would help find the way to deal with the hijackings."

SM: "How did the reporters react to that?"

DB: "We had established a good rapport with the news media with our press conferences. As the Final Reported noted, 'The Task Force took particular care to offer the same advantage to each press representative and to supply the same story no matter which media were served.' A few reporters complained that I had destroyed their 'scoop' about how they beat a full-proof system. One reporter even said to me, 'This is the first time I ever heard a press officer admit the govemment had a system that was not perfect.' Of some 200 stories, only six were negative."

SM: "Sounds like a very smooth operation."

DB: "Actually, we almost never got off the ground, so to speak. Lowell was suspicious of me from the start because he had experienced some run-ins with reporters while he was in the Navy. He said out loud that I probably would blab everything to reporters. However, after our first trip, he saw the positive media reaction, and we became close friends after that. I honestly do not recall whose idea it was, but I was given a black-and-white videotape recorder and told to film passenger reaction. That turned the corner for an eventual all-gate all-airline test at New Orleans in mid-1970."

SM: "How long after your initial visit would you set up your test?"

DB: "Usually a couple of weeks. We would start at 7 am. to set up the equipment and get things in order for the day's flights. I usually held a press conference in mid-afternoon so the television stations would have stories for the evening news programs. Around 7 p.m., we would pack up and return to our hotel to discuss what we had learned. We found varying reasons airline passengers took trips to and from different locations. That helped Dr. Dailey tailor his behavioral characteristics depending on the airport. Some airport terminals had different configurations, so the magnetometer locations in the security areas would have to be flexible.'"

SM: "Anything else you learned?

DB: "Oh, yes. The Task Force arranged to produce airport signs warning of searches. I contacted the Voice of America to provide us with a Spanish translation. One day, I received a call from a San Diego airport official who pointed out that the Spanish translation we had provided was not the Spanish spoken in that area. So, we had to have two different translations."

SM: "That must have been embarrassing."

DB: "Well, it was unexpected. But then, so was the revelation that the Department of Agriculture maintained an inspection station at the San Juan airport that could double as our screening agent. We also discovered that Customs Bureau agents also operated at other airports, and they too could act as passenger screeners."

SM: "And, you followed the same routine at all the airports?"

DB: "Yes. After each one, Dr. Reighard gathered the Task Force members for a full-blown exchange of information and conclusions."

SM: "And, what were the conclusions?"

DB: "Perhaps the most startling one came when Dr. Dailey analyzed the data we had collected and concluded that no more than 2 percent of Eastern passengers fit-enough of the profile at most airports, and as low as 5-tenths of 1 percent at the others."

SM: "What was the significance of that?"

DB: "It told us that if we could concentrate on no more than 2 percent of the flying public, we had a chance of realistically coping with aircraft hijackings. No, we were not ignoring the other passengers. As I said before, we wanted the other 98 percent cleared for boarding as efficiently as possible. And, we wanted a pre-boarding procedure that had the best chance for success."

CHAPTER EIGHT —
THE OPPOSITION

SM: "Did the team feel the airlines would buy your concept?"

DB: "The obvious question was whether our data would be the same with airlines other than Eastern. The only way to do that was to pick a new airport and involve every airline there."

SM: "And, that airport was . .

DB: "New Orleans."

SM: "How were you going to get the other airlines to go along with that?"

DB: "The senior vice presidents of all the airlines servicing New Orleans were called into a meeting in the FAA's administrator's 9th floor conference room. When our team entered the room, those executives were seated around the oval-shaped table glaring at us. Mike Fenello, Eastern's senior vice president and literally our 'god father,' called the meeting to order. But, before he could go on, one of the other senior vice presidents stood up and said he had a statement to make on behalf of his colleagues."

SM: "Did you feel that was good news or bad news?"

DB: "Bad."

SM: "What did that executive say?"

DB: "He announced that the airlines had commissioned the Menninger Institute, that internationally known psychiatric center in Minnesota, to evaluate what we were doing."

SM: "And?""

DB: "He said the Menninger empirical analysis 'supported our conclusion that your system will put us out of business because passengers will be afraid to go through the search process before they board their flights.'"

SM: "What was the Task Force reaction to that?"

DB: "Fenello called on Dr. Reighard and Dr. Dailey to detail the results of our work. When that did not seem to sway the airline executives, Fenello disclosed that I had videotaped all the tests, and without exception, passengers were willing to be searched because at least the government was trying to do something positive, especially a United Nations diplomat. When Fenello asked if they would like to see the tapes, along with a stack of news stories lauding our testing, you could have heard a feather hit the floor. Then, he said he would take that to mean there not any objection to having us equip all airlines at New Orleans as a final test. There was unanimous agreement"

SM: "Sounds brave, but weren't you literally putting all your eggs in one basket?"

DB: "Absolutely. But, Dr. Reighard said he had full confidence in Dr. Dailey's profile, and was satisfied that our testing had produced a viable procedure if the profile were Step One. When word got back to some of our superiors, they complained that we could be endangering the reputation of the FAA. We felt the risk was not as great as feared, based on the passengers' reaction. Also, the media were supportive, even though there were those stories speculating on how the procedure could be breached."

SM: "And, could it be breached?"

DB: "Of course. We maintained all along no system is perfect. When I was a cub reporter in a small Ohio town, I mentioned to a police sergeant that I was flabbergasted at hearing that a robber tried to hold up a bank in another city despite an armed guard and a security camera in the lobby. The sergeant told me the robber did not expect to be caught. I could not believe his answer. He replied that I did not think like a criminal, that I was too logical. *That is exactly what I think is wrong today. We do not think like Mideast terrorists. We continue to be 'surprised' when those terrorists change their tactics.*"

SM: "Don't tell me that all the publicity stopped hijacking attempts?"

DB: "The publicity was part of a psychological approach Dr. Dailey carefully crafted. He said putting obstacles in the way often deters criminals. And, hijackings stopped during our publicized testing period."

SM: "Any other effect the publicity had?"

DB: " It had one almost comical side effect we had not considered. It turned out that the profile also fit drug dealers, law breakers, illegal aliens, and so forth. I had a call from an Eastern Airline gate manager at LaGuardia who complained that his crews were discovering discarded weapons and drugs in potted plants near the gates. He even said, in a low voice, that since Mafia members flew Eastern to Florida, our work would discourage them. We did hear that drug dealers became convinced that the profile was only aimed at them."

SM: "You have got to be kidding me!"

DB: "Truth be told, that is what happened."

SM: "Any other unexpected side effects of the testing?"

DB: "One internal one. In return for Dr. Reighard's support for my openness with the news media, I said I would ask the team for help in formulating answers to reporters' technical questions. Also, I offered to coach any Task Force member so he could speak accurately to a reporter without having to clear with me because we all would provide the same answers. However, my superior went ballistic when I told him about my approach, and he insisted that all media calls would have to go through him. He never asked me to brief him, however."

SM: "'Let's get back to the final test at New Orleans."

CHAPTER NINE

ALL OUR EGGS ARE IN ONE BASKET

DB: "Lowell, Max, and I did our usual trial run at New Orleans, and the others on our team coordinated with the airlines. With Dr. Reighard's approval, I contacted the local and national electronic and print media about the test. That was July of 1970. The airlines would choose the spokesman for a Thursday press conference."

SM: "Weren't you going to conduct it as you had done in the past?"

DB: "'Oh, no. Now, it was an airline show. I just coordinated the press alert. The news media were free to observe all the gates in operation and interview any passengers."

SM: "How did things go?"

DB: "Not as smooth as I thought they would. I had planned to fly down to New Orleans on that Monday with Lowell and Max. Dr. Dailey was to join us later. I had notified the media that I would be there on Monday. The Friday before, my superior called me into his office and said I could not leave until Tuesday, and that I had to be back in the office on Friday. Lowell, Max, and I had planned to take official leave on Friday and fly our wives down for a relaxing weekend."

SM: "What's that line about 'best laid plans' . . .?"

DB: "That's a line from a Robert Bums' poem... 'the best laid plans of mice and men oft go awry.' Anyhow, the only telephone call I received all day was from an angry Ike Papas, correspondent for the

Walter Cronkite television news show on CBS. He demanded to know why I wasn't in New Orleans to brief him. I gave him a lame excuse and said I would meet with him on Tuesday. He warned me that 'you had better be here, or my Thursday piece won't be one you like.'"

SM: "How did you handle that?"

DB: " I located Lowell and asked him to literally hold Ike's hand and give him as much as we could short of security. After all, a bad report on a major television news program would sink us so deep we never would recover."

SM: "So, you missed the press conference?"

DB: "Not only the press conference, but also the evening television news shows. Just before the press conference was to begin, I bumped into what seemed to be a still grumpy Papas. He told me he would wrap up his report right where I was standing, but he did not want me anywhere in sight. I was about to head back to the hotel and pack up when the correspondent for the Huntley-Brinkley news show on NBC saw me and apologized for getting to New Orleans only the day before. I said I was sorry for not being able to brief him, but he replied he got what he needed, and would stay for the press conference. So, here were two major television news shows that I felt I had shortchanged."

SM: "I get the impression you saw your career flashing before your eyes."

DB: "Did I ever. At the time both tv news programs were airing, I was on the plane headed home. I had called my wife earlier and asked her to watch both news shows. When I arrived around 8 p.m., she asked me if I was considering a career move. I stopped dead in my tracks, until she smiled and said we got glowing reports on both programs, especially Ike's report."

SM: "What happened when you got to the office the next day?"

DB: "My superior never said a word. I spent the day doing my travel report. The only telephone call I received came as I was about to go home for the day. It was from a top aide to Department of Transportation Secretary John A. Volpe, whom I also had alerted. He said sternly that Mr. Volpe wanted to see the Task Force in his office the following Tuesday morning."

SM: "I guess you were somewhat apprehensive?"

DB: "That's an understatement. I was scared stiff. I asked the caller for a clue for the meeting. He paused long enough for me to sweat, then said that the Secretary had watched both programs and wanted to know how we got such good coverage for a project he never had been briefed about. He gave us a full hour, and was very complimentary."

SM: "Mr. Brown, I'm sorry but I have another appointment shortly. You really seem to have information we have not been able to find elsewhere. Can we resume this tomorrow at the same time?"

DB: "I'm more than happy to do it. And, thank you for asking me back."

CHAPTER TEN —
DIRE PREDICTIONS

SM: "Thanks for continuing our dialogue despite interruptions. Where did we leave off.?"

DB: "We had briefed Secretary Volpe."

SM: "'Oh, yes. What happened after that?"

DB: "Essentially, our work was done. But, before the Task Force was disbanded, we all sat down in Dr. Reighard's conference room and began to formulate some conclusions."

SM: "What were they?"

DB: "We discussed whether potential hijackers would continue to be deterred by our maximum publicity stating that various search procedures were going to be in place. As I mentioned before, we all agreed that an individual terrorist, or a group of terrorists, would try to find ways to defeat any pre-boarding procedure. We believed that determined terrorists would even try to shoot their way onto an airplane if they had to."

SM: "Was that addressed in your Final Report?"

DB: "Well, the Report contains three prophetic warnings about the future. For example, Page 39 states: 'There are too many people in too many parts of the world with motivations for violence to argue against expectations that (airplane hijackings) would not only spread but become differentiated in character.' On Page 88, you can find this observation: ' . . . as times, people, motivations, and methods of operation change, a continuing research ... would be needed to meet challenges already on the horizon.' But, Page 93 has what I feel is the definitive prediction: 'The Task Force was aware that mass hijacking of U.S. aircraft could also be carried out by an organized group in order to achieve terrorist activities.' Keep in mind these preceded 9/11 by 23 years. But, there was one more aspect."

SM: "What was that?"

DB: "Let me quote from Page 72 of our Final Report: 'Analysis of intelligence data available suggested that both the FAA and the air carrier industry would be well advised to prepare for possible future all out attacks on American air carrier transportation.'"

SM: "The Commission seems to conclude that intelligence gathering was dysfunctional."

DB: "Be that as it may, all I can point out is that quote came in our 1978 Final Report. That is why I made the statement that disbanding the Task Force in 1970 destroyed a vital link between then and now."

CHAPTER ELEVEN —
SKY MARSHALS

SM: "Let me go back a bit to something you said earlier. So far, we have been talking about pre-boarding procedures. What about dealing with a hijacker, or hijackers, once the plane is in the air?"

DB: "One of the first things we did was to look carefully at how Israelis dealt with hijackers in the air. Our conclusion was that the United States was not prepared to take the same steps as found in El Al Airlines incidents. That is, armed guards were not afraid to shoot, even if it meant civilian casualties."

SM: "How else can you deal with this situation?"

DB: "We reasoned that we also would have to look at other onboard procedures in the event a terrorist, or group of them, got by the pre-boarding screening system. Using armed guards was one option. That brings me to the sky marshal alternative."

SM: "I had heard that airlines do use armed guards dressed as ordinary passengers."

DB: "Actually, the first effort in those says was to train military personnel to perform that task. In fact, I was assigned to be the spokesman for the first 'graduates' at a Fort Dix, New Jersey press conference."

SM: "Why you?"

DB: "It was a combination of my work with the Task Force, and my being an Army Reserve public information officer. As such, I was able to work closely with the military to carefully formulate what we would tell the media."

SM: "How did that work out?"

DB: "As is my lot, things began well, and then sank like a lead balloon."

SM: "What do you mean by that?"

DB: "I was in the middle of my presentation when I noticed a high-ranking Department of Transportation official walking up to the podium. He was not supposed to be part of the conference, but I had briefed him several weeks before because one of his responsibilities now that the Task Force was disbanded was to oversee the hijacking deterrence program. Obviously, he wanted to take over the press conference, so I did not have any choice but to introduce him."

SM: "How did that go?"

DB: "At first, it went well. He was saying the same words I had used in his briefing. Then, all of a sudden, he turned to me and asked whether we had any newly trained sky marshals on hand. I had to nod yes. He then ordered me to point them out. Well, doing that compromised these two men because their photos were all over the newspapers and on television. But, again, I did not have any choice. If that were not enough, he began talking about the weapons they would use. We did not want to reveal the special ammunition had been developed that would not damage the interior of any aircraft. He then ordered the two men to display those bullets. I was trying to back away when he told me to conclude the press conference, and walked away beaming. My military counterpart came over, patted me on the shoulder, and said he knew this was not my doing, that certainly I had been caught off guard. But I will admit to this. I caught up with the official and told him in no certain terms that he had destroyed a carefully planned news conference, had compromised two potential sky marshals, and had discussed a topic we wanted to avoid - the prospect of gun play at 35,000 feet in the air."

SM: "And, what was his reaction before he fired you?"

DB: "Would you believe he apologized to me? But, when I got back to my office, and after my superiors had seen the newspaper and television reports, there was no witness to his apology. I had to take the rap, but no, I did not get fired."

SM: "Tell me more about the sky marshal program"

DB: "After the Office of Air Transportation Security replaced our Task Force, an interim force of 800 soldiers was augmented by some 500 agents from the Bureau of Customs, the Secret Service, and the FBI were trained as sky marshals. Personnel from such Federal agencies as the National Park Service, the Fish and Wildlife Service, and the Postal Services also were trained under the Bureau. At one point, there were as many as 1,200 sky marshals traveling on random flights. But, as the years rolled on, the use of sky marshals diminished. Then, in 1985, Congress passed the International Security and Development Cooperation Act which validated the Federal Air Marshal program. In the interest of security, the FAA would not say how many sky marshals were in use, nor who they were. Nor would the agency reveal which flights they were on, or how they were trained."

SM: "That seems to follow along the approach you used with the media."

DB: "It was. But, here is a tidbit I got online from what was called The Marshals Monitor, the official site for the U.S. Marshals Service, part of the Department of Justice. There was one very interesting sentence that bears notice."

SM: "And, what was that?"

DB: "The sentence read: 'Legal guidelines stated that in order to perform a weapon search, there must be the solid belief that the person being searched could cause harm with the weapon and could cause a genuine fear for safety.' That was based on the Terry v Ohio case, which I would like to save for another time because it requires a lot of detail."

SM: "Okay. Let's continue with the sky marshal issue."

DB: "On January 14, 2002, the Los Angeles Times ran a story reporting that the sky marshal force has shrunk to 32 from a high of about 2,000 prior to 9/11. The story also stated that the force now had a goal of at least 2,000 sky marshals. It also asserted that on 9/11, sky marshals 'were in the wrong places - assigned to selected high-risk international flights, not domestic flights like the transcontinental routes targeted by Al Qaeda.' If that were not bad enough, the story quoted Douglas Laird, formerly head of security at Northwest Airlines, as claiming, 'What the government is doing is promoting a program to make people feel good.' To its credit, the story balanced this with a quote from O.K. Steele, former head of the FAA's security office, who asserted: ' . . . (the sky marshal program) has a deterrent effect.'"

SM: "Sounds like there certainly was turbulence in the program."

DB: "On August 10, 2003, The Miami Herald had an article reporting that some minority sky marshals claimed they were subjected to unfair treatment, including harassment."

SM: "I'm almost afraid to ask if there were any other problems."

DB: "MSNBC reported in July 2003 that the TSA was pulling sky marshals from some crosscountry and international flights 'because of budget problems associated with the costs of overnight lodging' for them."

SM: "What else could go wrong?"

DB: "You mean other than there not being an instance of sky marshals nabbing any Mideast terrorist hijackers? In 2003, the FAA issued a warning that several private firms in the West were illegally offering sky marshal training courses. The warning noted that sky marshals must be FAA employees. The warning added that some of the 'graduates' were issued a phony sky marshal badge, but had to buy their own weapons. The FAA never hired any of them."

SM: "I hope you do not have any more problem stories to relate."

DB: " Other than the complaints from many sky marshals about the boredom of cross-country and transoceanic flights, there is the fact that unfortunately the sky marshal program has a history of turbulence all along the way."

SM: "Again with the puns. But, okay, explain what you mean."

DB: "After the Department of Homeland Security was created after 9/11, one of its agencies was the Transportation Security Administration, which consolidated the government-wide airport security responsibility. The FAA's Office of Civil Aviation Security, as it was now called, was one of those folded into the TSA. On June 19, 2002, The Washington Post ran a story stating that members of the Federal Air Marshal Service, the sky marshals if you will, wanted to leave the TSA and join the new Bureau of Immigration and Customs Enforcement, although both were under TSA. They felt, according to the story, that they did not want to be in the same group as security officers who only worked at pre-boarding gates. Perhaps also contributing to this strife was a USA Today story a year earlier that claimed sky marshal applicants received curtailed training."

SM: "In reading your book, I was intrigued with your meeting with J. Edgar Hoover of the FBI that relates to security jurisdiction."

DB: "I had been transferred to the parent Department of Transportation News Division when I learned that there would be a press conference in Attorney General John Mitchell's office clarifying the responsibility of dealing with hijackers when a plane was still on the ground. The FBI would have the jurisdiction on the ground; the Department of Transportation would have the responsibility once the plane was in the air."

SM: "Where does Hoover come into all of this?"

DB: "I was talking with some of the reporters I had known when I worked for Attorney General Ramsey Clark when out of the corner of my eye I saw Hoover enter the room through a rear door. I expected to see his close aide, Clyde Tolson, with him. Then, I remembered that Tolson was on sick leave, part of a long illness. I must admit I thought this is a moment I cannot lose, so I walked over to Hoover who stood there alone. I introduced myself, explaining I had worked with my FBI counterpart Tom Bishop. Hoover lied when he said he remembered me now. But, here I was, chatting it up with Hoover, one on one, the rarest of opportunities. I never heard anyone having that opportunity ever."

SM: "Okay, you've got my attention now. What then?"

DB: "I asked Hoover if he had met the high-ranking Department of Transportation official who would be taking part in the press conference with him. He said no. I responded that I knew the official and would be happy to introduce Hoover to him. So, we walked over to the middle of the room where the official was standing. The talking stopped immediately when the reporters saw Hoover."

SM: "Is there some point to this?"

DB: "After I introduced the two, I backed off. A short time later, Ron Ostrow, the Los Angeles Times reporter who had covered the Justice Department when I worked there, rushed over to me and said, 'You S.O.B., why didn't you tell me you had an in with Hoover? I've been tying to interview him for eight years.'"

SM: "What was your response to that?"

DB: "I said, 'Ron, why didn't you ask me?' Truthfully, that was my first and only encounter with the infamous FBI director. That Department of Transportation official was the same one who ruined that sky marshal press conference at Fort Dix."

SM: "Let's get back to the sky marshals. How did the Task Force feel about armed officers on flights?"

DB: "Dr. Dailey and I were in the minority that felt this was not a feasible alternative."

SM: "Why not? It seems to have worked for the Israelis."

DB: "First of all, El Al has infinitely fewer flights than all U.S. airlines. Second, checking out potential terrorist hijackers in the Mideast was much simpler. And, third, the Mideast always seems to be on military alert. As I said before, we felt this was not an acceptable alternative for U.S. flights."

SM: "Any other reasons for your minority opinion?"

DB: " Dr. Dailey and I tried to point out that with some 30,000 flights a day throughout the U.S., it would take an army of marshals to protect each and every flight. Those guards would be subject to the same number of flying hours as flight crews, also meaning putting up with long times away from families. And, who would pay for all the increased costs that would result?"

SM: "But, I got the impression you had other approaches to in-flight measures."

CHAPTER TWELVE —
AIRBORNE PROTECTION

DB: "There was a cockpit device that was 100 percent lethal. We only saw a highly classified film of it, and we were horrified. Had that device been installed on the hijacked airplanes on 9/11, the terrorists would have died, allowing the U.S. cockpit crews to regain control of their aircraft."

SM: "Can you tell me more about that?"

DB: "No, I am afraid I can't. We were literally sworn to secrecy, and to my knowledge, it still is secret to this day."

SM: "But, if this device, whatever it was, was so good, why didn't the airlines install it?"

DB: "They were briefed on it, but for whatever reason, none decided to use it. Besides, the number of hijackings greatly diminished, so I would assume the airlines felt let well enough alone. But, one of the things we did accomplish, that had not been on our agenda, was the work of Lowell Davis."

SM: "What was that?"

DB: "You won't believe how simple it really was. Lowell always had been safety minded. He was the one who got the airlines to paint outlines of the exterior aircraft doors. He realized that during crashes, rescuers had a difficult time finding the exit doors. Even more than that, he was the one who insisted early on that cockpit doors needed to be more secure. Not only were too many doors flimsy, but they often were left open during some takeoffs."

SM: "That seems almost too simple."

DB: "Maybe so, but the cockpit door change has done more to protect the cockpit crew than almost anything else."

SM: "But, didn't the 9/11 terrorists get into the cockpits?"

DB: "Obviously, those cockpit doors could be breached at that time. To repeat, determined terrorists will use any means to accomplish their mission."

SM: "Well, if you have armed guards on board, they should be able to deal with in-flight problems."

DB: "Would you be surprised to learn that a year after our group was disbanded that a hijacker forced an American Airlines B-747 to Havana despite the fact that three air marshals and an FBI agent were on board?"

SM: "What about arming the cockpit crew?"

CHAPTER THIRTEEN —
ARMING PILOTS

DB: "That is another issue where Dr. Dailey and I occupy the minority seat. Most aircraft cockpits are not 5-star hotel room size. They are crammed with instruments. Besides, while the plane is in the air, the captain and copilot are strapped into their seats. Let's say a hijacker got entry into the cockpit. Let's say the plane is on autopilot. Even if the left-seat captain can reach his shoulder holster, how is he or she going to be able to turn around enough to get a clear shot at the intruder? And, even if the right-seat copilot can draw his or her weapon, how is he or she going to be able to turn around enough to get a clear shot at the intruder? The fact is that the majority of pilots do not want to carry weapons because the chances of them being able to use their weapons effectively are not in their favor."

SM: "What about the hijacked flight that crashed in Pennsylvania?"

DB: "That effort by passengers to try to overpower the terrorists was courage rare in history. Everyone was going to die anyhow. But, to me, that validates our efforts to focus on keeping those people off the aircraft in the first place. And, I will not stop from emphasizing how important Dr. Dailey's profile is in identifying potential Mideast terrorists before they board."

SM: "How did you and Dr. Dailey feel about being in the minority?"

DB: "There continues to be much controversy over this subject. Let me start with the Department of Homeland Security first. On

June 4, 2002, the Government Executive Magazine reported that TSA Director John Magaw told the Senate Commerce Committee: 'It's clear in my mind, when I weigh all of the pros and cons, pilots should not have firearms in the cockpit. If something does happen on that plane, they really need to be in control of that aircraft.' Yet, the same story noted that because there were not enough sky marshals to ride every flight, 'many members of Congress believe that armed pilots are a much better line of defense.'"

SM: "Sounds convincing."

DB: "The TSA and the Air Line Pilots Association agree with arming pilots. The article noted that ALPA points out armed pilots can defend the cockpit from inside, while sky marshals cannot. But, on the other hand, the Department of Transportation is against arming the cockpit crew, as are many pilots. Yet, a Los Angeles Times story in June 1972 stated that 'some captains believe that a gun at the head of the pilot is the greatest risk aloft.' On the other hand, the same story noted that other pilots claim 'a threat to a stewardess would be quite as effective as a gunman in the cockpit.'"

SM: "It just occurred to me that there might be a situation where the pilot is armed and there also are armed sky marshals on board."

DB: "I guess that is like an airborne version of the 1957 movie 'Gunfight at the OK Corral.' I don't mean to be flip about this, but yes, that could be a possibility. Anything could be possible. It is my understanding that the captain always is informed if an armed officer is on board. Again, this continues to support the Task Force conclusion that the greatest effort should be focused on keeping Mideast terrorists off the flight in the first place. By the way, a congressional report in 2003 revealed that two terrorists sneaked past security at a New York airport as a videotaped dry run well before 9/11. On 9/11, they sneaked box cutters aboard their flights."

SM: "What about other countries around the world? What is their view of arming pilots?"

DB: "The operative word seems to be caution. Of course, Israel has done it for years, in addition to uniformed guards. The BBC reported that England's Virgin Airlines preferred 'strengthening and protecting the security of the flight deck (read that to mean the cockpit door) and enhancing the screening and profiling of passengers and baggage.'"

SM: "Do I understand that pilots and crews are asked to report suspicious behavior?"

DB: "I came across that in a USA Today story in January 2004. The problem is that there does not seem to be an international data base to sift through all such information to give pilots an accurate warning of danger. And, there always is the danger that 'suspicious' actions can trigger unwarranted security action."

SM: "Didn't your book cite an example of that?"

DB: " You're referring to the Delta Flight 442 incident out of Atlanta in 2002. I use as my reference a story in the September 19, 2002 edition of The Philadelphia Inquirer. Two sky marshals were on board the flight to Philadelphia when a passenger was seen going through other people's luggage in the overhead bins. Their dealings with him led to another incident. Then, things got complicated. The marshals handcuffed the unruly man, rushed him to first-class, and pushed him into aisle Seat 1-C. The passenger in window Seat 1-D, a man of Indian descent but dressed in typical American clothing, had been reading a book. When he noticed what was happening, he stood up and asked to be moved. When one marshal sat down in 1-D to guard the unruly man, a flight attendant seated the passenger where the marshal had been. Meanwhile, back in the coach class, a woman wanted to switch seats with another woman on the aisle. For some reason, the second marshal must have thought this somehow was related to the handcuffed passenger. The marshal suddenly appeared at the partition dividing first-class from the coach section and, according to eye witnesses, he drew his pistol and ordered: 'Nobody move, nobody look down the aisle, nobody takes pictures or you will go to jail, nobody do anything.'"

SM: "Like I said, this sounds like a television movie."

DB: "One eye witness was Philadelphia Common Please Court Judge James Lineberger."

SM: "Now, that's an eye witness."

DB: "About half an hour later, the plane landed in Philadelphia. No sooner had the cabin door opened when local police officers came aboard to help the one marshal take the handcuffed prison off the plane. Finally, the passengers began to stand up, expecting to get off the plane. Before anyone could disembark, the second marshal went over to where the Indian man was sitting in first-class and ordered, 'Head down, hands over your head!' He was handcuffed and whisked off to the airport police station. Ironically, the woman who had been involved in the incident in coach was the Indian man's wife. She could not get a seat in first-class, so the couple had to be separated."

SM: "Are you sure this is not a television movie?"

DB: "Things got worse in a hurry. The Indian man was placed into a cell he later described as so filthy 'I wouldn't even put my dog in it.' The officers demanded his name, address, and Social Security number. When he asked why he was being treated that way, he said one responded, 'We didn't like the way you looked at us.' He later would say he never looked up at either sky marshal. After three hours, he was told to leave. No explanation. He and his wife finally were reunited."

SM: "Who was this Indian man?"

DB: "His name was Dr. Robert Rajcoomar, a naturalized U.S. citizen since 1985. He had been a medical major in the Army, and currently had been in private practice for nearly two decades."

SM: "Did the doctor sue? I would have."

DB: "I honestly do not know. But, I'll bet the ACLU heard about it."

SM: "Okay, let's get back to that profile."

CHAPTER FOURTEEN

THE PROFILE AND THE LAW

D B: "Dr. Dailey told the Task Force the only way our system would pass legal muster was a multi-step procedure with the profile as the initial phase. Information gathered before passengers got to the boarding gate, at the time they got their tickets, and even before they boarded, had to be combined with modem technology to be what he described as a screening system that 'is both *maximally effective* and *minimally intrusive.*' In my first book, Dr. Dailey asserted that 'since the system used today is *minimally effective* but *maximally intrusive*, it is a farce because innocent nonthreatening airline passengers are subjected to long and unnecessary personal searches.'"

SM: "You tested his profile, I assume, because it was just a theory."

DB: "That theory, as you term it, gained the approval of the American Civil Liberties Union because the profile did not involve 'racial screening.' In addition, a New York Federal Court judge ruled that Dr. Dailey's profile did not violate the Fourth Amendment to the Constitution."

SM: "Isn't that the one dealing with search and seizure? Explain that court ruling."

DB: "Actually, there are two key court decisions. The one you are referring to was the case of *United States of America v. Frank Lorenzi Lopez*. Lopez and a companion, Gonzales, were about to board a Pan American Airways flight out of JFK International Airport headed for Puerto Rico on November 14, 1970 when a gate agent determined the two men fit enough of Dr. Dailey's profile to be detained. Also, the two men set off the magnetometer. They then refused to produce valid identification. Following our tested procedure, the men were ordered back through the detector. Again, they set if off. Lopez and his friend were taken to a private area where they were 'patted down.' Although no weapons were found, a plastic envelope under Lopez's clothing turned out to be heroin."

SM: "What set off the detector?"

DB: "Lopez's friend had a small bag, which apparently contained some metal. But, there was nothing suspicious in it."

SM: "So, what was there in this court case that resulted in such an important ruling?"

DB: "Of all the ironies, the Pan Am service manager on his own issued a memorandum four months earlier to what he called 'updating' Dr. Dailey's list of characteristics. However, in doing so, the manager eliminated one of the fundamental characteristics of potential hijackers that Dr. Dailey had described privately to the judge, and added one that introduced what the record stated was 'an ethnic element ... raising serious equal protection problems. That added element called for individual judgment.' As a result, the judge ruled that the seized heroin could not be considered evidence."

SM: "Are you telling me the ruling turned on a technicality?"

DB: " Yes, but - and that is a big but - the judge ruled that the effect of the changes 'was to destroy the essential neutrality and objectivity of the approved profile.' In other words, the judge validated Dr. Dailey's profile as long as there were no changes to it. Also, the judge explained that Dr. Dailey's profile 'can be a valuable and effective method of protecting millions of air travelers from the threat of violence and sudden death in the air.'"

SM: "That's quite a decision."

DB: "Ironically, Pan Am had the right idea in applying Dr. Dailey's profile as Step One. The airline just messed with a procedure that, to repeat myself, we tested at various airports."

SM: "You said there were two key cases. What was the other one?"

DB: "I found the courthouse library a fountain of information, as the saying goes, and the librarians were wonderful helpers once I announced I was not an attorney. That is how I discovered the case of *Terry v. Ohio*. According to court documents, on October 31, 1963, Cleveland detective Martin McFadden claimed he saw two men presumably 'casing' a store. He approached the two men, told them he was a police officer, and asked their names. One was John W. Terry, and the other Richard Milton. When they seemed nervous, McFadden searched them for weapons, which they both had. He arrested them for carrying concealed weapons, and they later were sentenced to three years in prison. Terry appealed his conviction, arguing through his attorney that his arrest violated the Fourth Amendment to the Constitution regarding search and seizure. The appeal went to the U.S. Supreme Court, which ruled that the officer was within his rights because he had 'reasonable suspicion that the person stopped is committing a crime, or is about to.' To me, the vital words in that decision are 'reasonable suspicion.' Remember that the *Lopez* decision turned on a technicality - that the gate agent had changed a vital element in Dr. Dailey's profile. This overrode the proper 'reasonable suspicion' exercised by the gate personnel. Had the profile not been significantly changed, the verdict would have been very different. In my book, I cited the 1973 Federal American Law Review noting, 'Had the decision to stop and frisk (Lopez and Gonzalez) been made solely on the basis of activating the magnetometer, the court might have reached a different result.' In kind of a reverse finding, the judge on the one hand agreed that the *Terry* decision was properly applied, but without proper 'reasonable suspicion' either by Dr. Dailey's proper profile or the metal detector, he had no choice but to agree that any evidence found on the defendants had to be suppressed. And, once that evidence could not be used, Lopez won his appeal."

SM: "There must be other cases dealing with the Fourth Amendment and passenger search."

DB: "Lots. In *Chandler v. Miller*, the case revolved around a Georgia law requiring candidates for state office to pass a drug test. Miller refused to take one, claiming it was in essence a search without suspicion. The U.S. Supreme Court agreed with his appeal."

SM: "Well, if suspicion has to be the first element for a constitutional search, how does that relate to airline passenger screening?"

DB: "Excellent question. I wondered about that myself. I felt that ordering every airline passenger to be searched only on the basis of setting off the magnetometer was improper. That goes back to Dr. Dailey's profile. We felt that if a passenger fit at least half a dozen elements of the profile, that was basis for suspicion. In fact, we referred to them as 'suspects.' Only then did we feel the authorities could go to the next steps of the total security system. And, when we discovered that no more than 2 percent of Eastern passengers tested, we concluded the proper search procedure would not impede the prompt boarding of the other 98 percent. The Final Report noted that Pan American World Airways, Trans World Airlines, and Continental Airlines later began to use the screening system. 'Of the first 226,000 passengers screened by those three airlines, some 1,268 selectees were identified for *further checking*. This is something more than one-half of 1 percent. Of those, only 638 failed the magnetometer test and required interviews. Thus, only 28/100th of 1 percent of total passengers screened required an interview following profile and magnetometer application. Of those interviewed, over half were able to provide a satisfactory explanation for high magnetometer readings. The balance, 304, submitted to search voluntarily. Of the 638 interviewed, 24 were denied boarding - and most were placed under arrest for offenses relating to narcotics or concealed weapons violations.'"

SM: "That's pretty convincing statistical evidence."

DB: "By the same token, Dr. Dailey and I feel that the number of suspected Mideast terrorists could be only a fraction of 1 percent of the total flying public, and thus easier to set them aside for further search and interrogation. Little did I realize, until I did further research, that President Bush has the authority to get around that 'suspicion' requirement because of the conflicts in the Middle East."

SM: "Did you get legal support, like from the Department of Justice?"

DB: "As the Final Report noted, in March 1969, the Department notified the FAA that our proposed screening procedure, with the profile as Step One, 'appeared reasonable and would be full endorsed by its Criminal Division.' Not only that, but the Division as well as the U.S. Marshals Service, which comes under the Department, pledged full cooperation in providing liaison and assistance."

SM: "What about the FBI?"

DB: "We tried to get the FBI to take part in the screening and searching of passengers, but it refused. Instead, U.S. marshals readily accepted that role."

SM: "Were there other legal aspects bearing on search?"

DB: "In November 2001, the Senate Republican Policy Committee issued a lengthy press release aimed at the American Civil Liberties Union. It stated that in the Spring of 1973, the ACLU 'adopted an official policy that opposed the present and previous systems of airport searches because they violate the requirements of the Fourth Amendment.' As stated before, the ACLU approved Dr. Dailey's profile, but apparently it did not like the current search procedure. The release cited the ACLU as opposing 'the current practice of searching the persons and belongings of all individuals' as inconsistent with the Fourth Amendment.' Notice the emphasis on all. We got approved because we opposed searching everyone."

CHAPTER FIFTEEN —
THE PROFILE AND FLEXIB1LITY

SM: "So, if I understand you, the profile is what should provide the suspicion, not the magnetometer?"

DB: "In the interest of focusing on the most likely 'suspects,' absolutely yes.

SM: "And, if the most likely 'suspects' as you put it now are Mideast terrorists, that is why you and Dr. Dailey advocate changing the profile to meet the times?"

DB: " Absolutely! But, it has to be done using common sense. The Council on Foreign Relations published a paper posing this question: 'Do suicide terrorists fit a common profile?'"

SM: "What was the answer?"

DB: "The analogy of the Japanese kamikaze attacks during World War II is one answer. While our country had not experienced suicide terrorism on our soil as it pertains to aircraft hijacking prior to 9/11, certainly such terrorism in the Mideast should have alerted the U.S. to the possibility of such events happening to us. After all, terrorists bombed the World Trade Center in the early 1990's. That is why I said that disbanding the Task Force destroyed the historical connection between our work during 1969-70 and events three decades later."

SM: "So, you felt the new Office should have just continued on with what you began."

DB: "Since I was not part of that Office, I cannot say for sure. However, from what I understand, what eventually became the Office of Civil Aviation Security essentially was a 'cop shop.' Where the Task Force operated pretty much on its own, the new Office probably was a typical bureaucratic creation. The FAA has the reputation for being very passive until being pushed to do something. The attitude seems to be not to rock the boat, and do just enough to get a decent annual performance rating for shuffling paperwork. Eventually, it folded into the newly created Transportation Security Administration, part of the Department of Homeland Security."

SM: "By 1978, it must have seen your Final Report with its predictions."

DB: "You would think so. When I was researching my first book, I called that Office to ask that question. One person told me, 'Yeah, I've read it.' When I asked, 'Why didn't you dust it off when the World Trade Center was bombed in the early 1990's?' his reply was, 'Not my responsibility.' I will guarantee you that had our group been kept together, we would have been reviewing it constantly, especially those predictions. We were very proactive."

SM: "That sounds self-serving."

DB: "Of course I am biased. Dr. Dailey and I are angry that the FAA just sat there virtually doing nothing when the agency had in its hands a Manual of our work with those predictions. By destroying our link the past, the 'cop shop' would not know how flexible we were. For example, by going to those nine airports we discovered a variety of airport gates and a variety of types of passengers. Dr. Dailey always said his profile had to be adjusted from time to time. That is flexibility. I rest my case on that subject."

SM: "The 'cop shop' or whatever you call it must be doing something right."

DB: "Yes, of course. The screening per se is something right. However, no one has remembered that our approach not only was to spot 'suspects' but equally as important to facilitate boarding of 'innocent' passengers. Dr. Dailey and I have tried to contact almost all levels of government to help out on that. But, to no avail. That is why I am doing these books, in the hope that it is not too late to get proper passenger screening back to where it is efficient. Allow me to create a scenario that relates to what we have been saying."

SM: "I'm listening."

CHAPTER SIXTEEN —
THE GOOD, THE BAD, AND THE UGLY

DB: "The line of passengers waiting at the security station at Dulles International Airport was backed up. Screeners were focused on a white-haired woman in her 80's who slowly passed through the metal detector. The alarm went off, and she was told to go back through. She slowly returned to the front of the device and went through once more. The device sounded again."

"'Oh, dear,' she said to a screener. 'What did I do?'

"'Ma'am,' the screener said, 'go over that search area. A female officer will take you behind a curtain, where you should begin to ... ah ... disrobe.'

"The woman seemed confused. 'Why do I have to do that?' she asked, continuing to stand in front of the detector so no one else could get through.

"'Ma'am, you're holding up the line. Officer, please escort this woman so we can get the line moving.'

"A very overweight male officer took her elbow and directed to a small area to what looked like a curtained voting booth. A female office soon appeared and said, 'Please go inside and take off your outer clothing and shoes. I'll be back in a minute.' The now frightened woman did as she was told. A moment later, the female officer stepped inside the booth with her electronic wand, a hand-held version of the large metal detector. She ran the wand up and down the woman's body when it suddenly began to beep shrilly. 'Whatcha got there, honey?'

the officer asked. 'Oh, dear,' she replied, 'that must be my pacemaker. I do have a note from my doctor in my purse.' The officer ignored the response and finally finished the scan, including the shoes. 'Okay, you can get dressed now and go on through,' she explained.

"The woman's 90-year-old husband, who had been right behind her in line, was having his own troubles. He too set off the alarm. The same burly officer led him to another search area, where he would be put through the same procedure his wife had experienced. The hefty officer's wand screeched almost immediately. 'Oh, my,' the man said, 'I have a hip replacement. I have a note from my doctor...' The officer was not interested and ran the wand along the man's shoes. Again it screeched. 'What's in your shoes, old man?' the officer asked. 'Oh, that's my lift. I was born with one foot shorter than the other, and my doctor told me to have a steel piece put into the heel to even me out. But, that threw 'my hip out of joint, so that's why...'

"The officer walked away and called to his supervisor, who also did a scan with the same results. The two officers whispered to one another until the supervisor said, 'Sir, let's see some photo ID.' The man fumbled through his pants that lay crumpled on the floor and finally found his card from the senior citizens development where he and his wife lived. The supervisor looked at it closely, then at the man, then at the ID, then at the man. Finally, he called over to the shift captain. After yet another whispered conference, the captain said, 'Sorry to inconvenience you, sir, but you know that ever since that shoe bomber incident, we can't be too careful. You're free to go and join your wife.'

"As he dressed, the man did not have any idea who or what a shoe bomber was. Rejoining his wife, who was now trembling, they slowly walked down the concourse to their departure gate."

SM: "You ought to be writing for television, or the movies."

DB: "Actually, part of that was based on a true incident a neighbor of ours encountered."

SM: "Any other incidents?"

DB: "Here is more of what New York Times columnist Joe Sharkey reported in his May 3, 2005 piece: At the Albuquerque, NM Airport, a passenger had her 6-month-old infant in her arms when she was stopped and told to remove her long-sleeve shirt, although she said others in line were not told to do so. She was taken aside. While she was subjected to a full body search, she said her infant also got a 'pat-down' as well. Then, there was the elderly woman at the Springfield, MO Airport in a wheelchair who was told to remove her shoes and 'every piece of outer wear, including her sweater.' Then, she was wheeled through the metal detector. Finally, one woman passenger refused to remove her shoes. She finally did after getting an additional inspection. Then, as she walked to her gate, she said she noticed a 'plainclothes guy doing his best imitation of a surfer, except for his military posture and the earpiece wire poking out from his ski cap.'"

SM: "Those might be exceptions to the rule."

DB: "I am not sure anyone tracks complaints because most people just want to get to their destinations and be done with it, so they assume there is some rationale behind such treatment."

CHAPTER SEVENTEEN —
NO REPEAT OF 9/11

SM: "I understand you have made a number of observations about terrorism in general. I don't remember seeing or hearing you on any television talk shows. I can accept the fact that you have unique knowledge of airline passenger screening. But, aren't you going a bit far afield? For example, I understand that in a speech you gave on this subject, you said you doubted that there would be a repeat of 9/11."

DB: "That came in response to a question from someone in the audience. Truth be told, he was a skeptic about our program. In fact, he said he did not agree with one thing I said, and called me 'dangerous.' I said I felt strongly that Mideast terrorists would not try that method again. In a nutshell, there are many, many more what we used to call in the Army **targets of opportunity** on U.S. soil with a lot less risk than in trying again to hijack airplanes and divebomb them into buildings. We are such an open, and sometimes naive, society that we cannot hope to cover every possible target, the same way we cannot cover every one of the 30,000 daily flights in this country with armed sky marshals. Besides, those terrorists have a more immediate goal in Iraq and Afghanistan. And, as dysfunctional as our current system is, it still is a deterrent."

SM: "But, how do you account for the tragedies in London?"

DB: "If nothing else, that was in Europe where terrorists have the makings and the opportunities for suicide bombings. Also, London was totally unprepared for what happened. I am not saying that in a negative way. The point I am trying to make is that those terrorists, whether directly or indirectly connected with Al Qaeda, have a whole range of **targets of opportunity** with a risk of being caught less than trying to hijack an airplane."

SM: " Are you saying we are totally fair game?"

DB: "In a sense, yes. To my way of thinking, Mideast terrorists will keep doing their evil deeds until the risk factor is too great And, that goes for suicide bombings. But, I think we lose sight of the fact that such horrific events are as much propaganda for the dissident world as they are for us. One of my observations is that I feel Mideast terrorists are winning the psychological war. The very realization that they can strike anywhere in the world, even killing or maiming innocent adults and children, is chilling. Look at how many alerts have us near panic. So, what I am saying is that I feel those terrorists are looking at those other opportunities."

SM: "And, what are some of those so-called **targets of opportunity?**"

DB: "I think I would be guilty of disservice if I got specific. I can tell you this much. A number of people in the audiences where I have appeared have offered their own specifics. But, that begs another question. Can the U.S. exhibit the same resolve and resiliency the Londoners showed? Don't forget that London survived horrendous Nazi air strikes. We have not had to do that. Having said that, I like to quote President Franklin D. Roosevelt's famous words, 'The only thing we have to fear, is fear itself.' That is why I plead for sensible and effective antiterrorist programs that we can have confidence in."

SM: "In mid-2005, terrorists seemed to focus on bombing mass transit vehicles."

DB: "Not only that, but they kept up the pressure in Iraq and Afghanistan, and even turned to Egypt. From a tactical viewpoint, that points up the advantage those terrorists have over us. They know where to strike next, while we have to wait for the event to happen. They are not fighting fair. But, that is guerilla warfare, and as I said before, that is a type of warfare we are not used to fighting. I remember reading an article stating that the terrorists do not seem to have any problem in obtaining recruits, although there are reports that they have used coercion. That does not bother them. They will use any means to obtain their objective."

SM: "But, that's just your point of view."

DB: "The New York Times columnist Thomas Friedman also has the same point of view. In an April 13, 2005 piece, he noted: 'I've always believed that one of the most important reasons there has been no new terrorist attack in America has to do with the U.S. invasions of both Iraq and Afghanistan. To the extent that the (enemy) have a coordinated strategy (in those two countries), their first priority, I think, is to defeat American forces in the heart of their world. Because if they can defeat America in the heart of the Arab-Muslim world, it will have so much more resonance than setting off a car bomb in Las Vegas - especially now that 9/11 has set the terrorism bar so high in terms of effect.' He went on to say that if Iraq can form a freely elected government, 'that may signal the ... insurgency is being gradually defeated.... I fear that when and if the Jihadists conclude that they have been defeated in the heart of their world ... they may want to launch a spectacular, headline-grabbing act of terrorism in America that tries to mask, and compensate for, just how defeated they have become at home.'"

SM: "That's a pretty strong statement that seems to coincide with your views."

DB: "A friend of mine once said, 'If the Mideast terrorists want to make a statement, and they don't care about another 9/11, they might just try to attack a State Fair.'"

SM: "That's a scary speculation."

DB: "As I said, before they are too many easier targets of opportunity for Mideast terrorists if are as desperate as Friedman suggests. Should we stop the New Year's Eve celebration at Times Square? Should we stop the July 4th celebration on the national capital's Mall? Should we stop all athletic events? The list is endless. My answer is an emphatic NO! As Friedman ended his column, 'Let's stay extra vigilant at home.'"

CHAPTER EIGHTEEN —
THE DOLLAR DRAIN

SM: "I understand another observation is that the conflicts in Iraq and Afghanistan are draining us financially."

DB: "More correctly, I said I feel Mideast terrorism has succeeded in diverting billions of U.S. dollars from our domestic needs. I am not an economist by any stretch of the imagination, but I understand the need to balance the books of our nation. Using money for the military is vital, but it must be used wisely. We cannot ignore major internal problems at the cost of funding a seemingly unending conflict. I am reminded of U.S. Senator J. William Fulbright of Arkansas. If my memory is correct, this brilliant man, who lent his name not only to highly sought academic scholarships but many political accomplishments, was defeated by then Arkansas Governor Dale Bumpers because he was accused of spending too much time away from his home state and from the people who elected him."

SM: "And, as I have asked before, your point is?"

DB: "The point is that we can be rich on the global front, but poor on the domestic front. Trying to balance the two is a monumental task. From what I read and hear, this teeter-totter cannot remain balanced forever. I think one way to help with the balance is to redirect our antiterrorism activities in a more productive way. Just throwing more and more money at homeland security is not the answer. As with a successful business, there has to be fiscal accountability in those efforts. Yes, I am talking dollars and sense ... s-e-n-s-e, not c-e-n-t-s

... if you forgive the pun. I admit I am not a historian, but I will bet there are plenty of examples where so much money went for foreign warfare at the expense of needs of the folks back home that people rebelled. I am not implying anyone will rebel, because that would denigrate the loss of military lives."

CHAPTER NINETEEN —
AIRBORNE DISTRACTIONS

SM: "Let's get back once more to the profile, because another question just popped into my head about armed sky marshals versus an armed cockpit crew."

DB: "More are those who have argued that either arm one or the other, but not both. Besides, gunplay at 35,000 should be avoided unless the circumstances do not leave any alternative."

SM: "You said armed sky marshals could not be on every flight. Were there any on the 9/11 flights?"

DB: "No. Boston, where two of the flights left from, had not had hijackings for many, many years. Personally, I am very opposed to the theory that having such personnel on certain flights, but not others, is a viable deterrent. Anyone could easily figure out the chances of catching a Mideast terrorist this way presents worse odds than trying to win the Lottery. My first book cited the FAA's own Bureau of Transportation Statistics concluding that there are 677,000 to 878,00 what are called 'revenue departures' a month. That does not take into consideration small private planes or even cargo planes. The numbers just are not there."

SM: "Are you saying armed sky marshals are not worth it?"

DB: "What I am saying is that I do not think that is a realistic alternative. If Mideast terrorists were able to board a plane, I submit that an armed sky marshal would not deter them. Let me give you this scenario. Let's take one of those 9/11 flights with five Mideast terrorist hijackers on board. One of those terrorists would make a commotion, enough to alert an armed sky marshal if one were aboard. Now, the terrorists knew they were home free."

SM: "Oh, come on. Where did you make that up from?"

DB: "When my wife and I were in Nice, France years ago, an elderly small woman with a baby in her arms came up to us begging for some money. While I was trying to shoo the woman away, I suddenly turned around to find a young boy standing next to me with his hand in my pocket. In another second or two, he would have had my passport. Or, if you prefer, such diversions are the stock and trade for magicians."

SM: "This all sounds as if we don't have a chance at dealing with terrorist hijackers once the plane is in flight."

DB: "I think that is an oversimplification. But, I repeat myself when I say the odds of dealing with such people shift from being in our favor on the ground to being in their favor once the plane is in the air. And, the latter becomes worse if you have suicide terrorists, who will give up their own lives, and take the lives of others, to accomplish their mission."

SM: "You've made your point."

DB: "One last item. The situation in the air gets worse on behemoth aircraft like a B-747 which has double decks. The terrorists could create a diversion on the upper deck, and drawing armed guards away from the main cabin. And, today, even larger aircraft are coming into service."

SM: "Well, if you don't have enough sky marshals to go around, what's wrong with telling the public they could be on certain flights?"

CHAPTER TWENTY

RANDOM IS AS RANDOM DOES

DB: "I certainly am not a psychologist, but it seems to me if you go that certain flights route, you are raising false hope. And, let's say, a plane is hijacked and passengers and crew are killed, but the flight did not have a sky marshal aboard. I am not sure I would trust that airline again. What could a sky marshal, or even two, have done on those 9/11 flights? As I said, if I were one of the terrorists, I would have made sure we identified that armed officer. But, let's go a step further and talk about pre-boarding random searches."

SM: "Please do."

DB: "After that Philadelphia incident, I wrote a letter to the Transportation Security Administration complaining about my random search. Here is part of that response: 'This random element prevents potential terrorists from beating the system by learning how it operates. Leaving out anyone group, such as senior citizens or the clergy, would remove the random element from the system and undermine security. We simply cannot assume that all future terrorists will fit any particular profile.'"

SM: "That sounds as if the TSA does not think much of your profile."

DB: "You got that right. By the same token, I would like to ask the TSA just how many terrorists has that agency caught under its random search procedure. I also would like to know just how the security people decide just who is subject to that random search.

It is ludicrous to believe any of the 9/11 terrorists could have been deterred by the prospect of being picked at random to be searched. Do the Iraqi terrorists stop bombing vehicles because they are in an armed convoy?"

SM: "Obviously you do not think much of random searching."

DB: "Not at the cost of humiliating passengers for no good reason. Don't just take my word for it. In my book, I cited a comment by noted columnist and television talk show panelist Charles Krauthammer: 'Random searches are a ridiculous charade ... that not only gives a false sense of security, but, in fact, diminishes security because it wastes so much time and effort on people who are obviously no threat. Random searches are being done purely to defend against the charge of racial profiling.' Dr. Dailey responded to Krauthammer in a letter to the editor this way: 'Racial and ethnic screening can only produce illegal search.' There even are those who argue that random searches violate the Fourth Amendment to the Constitution. Remember, the Federal Court judge upheld Dr. Dailey's profile because it did not involve racial screening."

SM: "Surely there is some good to random searching, or the TSA would have abandoned it."

DB: "I think here is where you have to understand the bureaucracy. Once a program is put in motion, you would have to move heaven on earth to stop it. It is like a freight train that suddenly has gone out of control, and no one knows how to stop it. The Council on Younger Lawyers of the Federal Bar Association noted in its 1968 handbook on the Bill of Rights that personal search is allowed 'so long as it was reasonable.' I would like to hear how the TSA defines 'reasonable.' What was 'reasonable' about me to require the only search on a flight? I did not have any dangerous weapon on me or in my carry-on. Anything else about me would fall into the racial or ethnic categories. Let me cite another source that I used in my other book. W.R. LaFave is a widely known and respect writer on legal matters. He cited a slew of cases in his 3ʳᵈ edition of *Search and Seizure*. He supported use of the profile as Step One. But, he went even further: 'The anti-hijacking system (of ours) is unusual in that it provides statistics showing the precise probabilities involved.' Also, LaFave pointed out that most passengers do not know that they can refuse to be searched, but will be denied boarding. However, that certainly raises suspicion."

SM: "So, you absolutely insist on the profile being Step One."

DB: "If you rely primarily on the metal detector, I submit the device only is as effective as the person operating it. There have been many stories about how easily scanners get bored. Much effort has been put into replacing the magnetometer with more sophisticated electronics. In a March 11, 2003 editorial, however, The New York Times stated that 'the creating of a highly intrusive federal surveillance program raises serious privacy and due process concerns.' LaFave cited the case of *United States v. Albarado* in which the ruling stated that use of the magnetometer alone 'would not serve any valid purpose as a high percentage of passengers activate the device even if carrying innocuous items.' La Fave went on to say: 'It by no means follows, however, that the screening authorities should immediately proceed to frisk a person who has activated the magnetometer. Such a procedure would deprive the hijacker detection system of a characteristic which is essential to it being deemed a reasonable administrative search, namely, that the intrusions are no more severe than is necessary to produce acceptable results.' Now, that opens another can of legal worms because of the many ways the term 'acceptable results' can be defined. All in all, there are as many court cases on one side of the issue as there are on the other."

SM: "Do I infer from what you just said the justification for a personal search can be based solely on setting off the magnetometer?"

DB: "Yes, but you have to remember that the President has the authority to approve such search under the 'war' powers Congress granted the President."

SM: "Are you implying the government is relying too much on electronics?"

DB: "The government keeps trying. The latest is called a 'puffer,' that allows screeners to find nonmetallic bombs without physically inspecting passengers."

SM: "What have you got against such devices?"

DB: "I'm not against devices. I'm against using them as Step One to screen every single passenger. In the American Psychologist magazine of February 1975, Dr. Dailey and his colleague, Dr. Evan W. Pickrel, discussed the psychological contributions to defenses against hijacking. They asserted that of the 30 hijackings between January 1970 and February 1971, '87 percent would have been stopped at the boarding gate if the (Task Force) screening procedures had been used, but (they) were only voluntary at that time.' Think about that. The profile could have prevented almost 9 out of 10 hijackings. Yes, electronics is important, but only if they are used in conjunction with the profile."

SM: "I must admit that is impressive."

DB: "The article also noted that 'following World War Two, an airline in Alaska used to frisk passengers on some of its flights and take away all guns, knives, and alcoholic beverages. Many (of those) pilots carried guns as part of their regular flight equipment and (also) locked the cabin door. If passengers were heard to be fighting, the pilots sometimes donned oxygen masks and simply climbed to an altitude that put the passengers to sleep.'"

SM: "That is almost comical. But, I supposed, in Alaska anything can happen."

DB: "The Internet also provided me with another interesting comment A writer named Michael Hammerschlag wrote a piece titled 'Airline Security.' His observation was this: 'By definition, the chance that any single random security break is an actual terrorist is negligible, since terrorists are so infinitesimal a number.'"

SM: "The impression you champion is that privacy of the individual is more important than fighting potential terrorist hijacking."

CHAPTER TWENTY ONE

PRIVACY VERSES SECURITY NEEDS

DB: "No, I am just trying to find a realistic balance between the two. Just to remind you, the American Civil Liberties Union approved of Dr. Dailey's approach because it did not involve an invasion of privacy. And, that was upheld in the New York Federal Court case. Then, there was a ruling on September 9, 2003 by U.S. District Court Judge Alvin Hellerstein in a suit filed by families of those killed or wounded in the World Trade Center suicide attacks. In upholding the families' right to sue not only the makers of the crashed aircrafts but also owners of the twin towers, Judge Hellerstein ruled that 'negligent security screening might have contributed to the deaths of 3,000 people.'"

SM: "Sounds to me like which came first, the chicken or the egg situation."

DB: "It is, but that is why we went out of our way to create a procedure that would meet security requirements, yet would necessarily abuse the right to privacy, the right to oppose improper searches. Frankly, I think current procedures have fallen into the trap of putting security ahead of privacy when there really has been a viable alternative for more than three decades."

SM: "What do the courts have to say about this Catch 22 dilemma?"

DB: "I did a lot of research on that and found that courts have not been in agreement with one another. The right to search was upheld in the famous *Terry v. Ohio* case where the Supreme Court ruled that a policeman could frisk a person if he were convinced it was needed to 'protect himself and others from possible danger.' My nonlegal focus is on the words 'if he were convinced.' In my frisk at Philadelphia that I described earlier, no 'convincing' was involved; I was merely picked out because, as the security officer admitted, 'we have to search at least one person on each flight.' Was my privacy improperly invaded? You betcha."

SM: "But, you are not a lawyer."

DB: "As the old joke goes, 'no, I'm not, but I have other good habits.' Let me cite you another court ruling I used in my previous book. In *United States v. Scott*, the Supreme Court ruled that 'searches are to be judged by a standard of objective reasonableness.' Here we go on a legal technicality. Because of 9/11, our country went to war with Mideast terrorists. As such, it tacitly ordered everyone to be searched as a defense against further such acts. The argument is whether that meant the Fourth Amendment to the Constitution only covered 'peaceful' times when the right to privacy and protection against improper searches and seizures could take place. I certainly am not a qualified legal person, but I submit a tried and true search system could prevent such dilemmas. However, let me play devil's advocate. In my book, I cited another case, *United States v. Skipworth*, which concluded that 'reasonableness does not require that officers search only those who meet (the) FAA personality profile or who manifest signs of nervousness or who otherwise appear suspicious.' Just to flip the legal coin back again, I cited the case of *United States v. Cyzewski* that ruled that 'airport searches are reasonable insofar as they permit government agents to determine whether (a) suspect presents (an) immediate danger to air commerce.'"

SM: "So, who's right and who's wrong?"

DB: "That is not for me to say. Again, what I do say is to the point of boring repetition is that Dr. Dailey's profile, and the system's step-by-step procedure, avoids this dilemma because suspicion is raised through at least half a dozen behavioral characteristics. Did I exhibit at least half a dozen of those characteristics? No, yet I was singled out for search. Did that 80-year-old woman exhibit at least half a dozen of those characteristics? No, yet she was singled out for search only because her pacemaker set off the magnetometer. Did her 90-year-old husband . . ."

SM: "Okay, okay. In all honesty, we are aware of some, shall we say, inappropriate procedures used by security personnel."

DB: "Some of those problems are due to the personnel themselves. Some are due to the equipment. A July 9, 1985 story in The New York Times quoted a security expert Robert W. Deichert as saying, 'The equipment and procedures are available to stop hijackings and terrorism, but they are not applied adequately, nor is common sense.' Another security expert, Henry P. Reis-El Bara, said, 'The technology is there. The problem is that as in many other things, the security at airports is oriented more toward crisis management than long-term vigilance.' The article went on to assert that some security devices 'are too often poorly operated or maintained, that security quality varies widely, that the weakest links in the system are personnel responsible for security, that new technology is delayed because of lack of funding, and that the risk of terrorism can never be eliminated.' Then, there is the observation in our Final Report on Page 6 'that human error or carelessness in use of deterrents might permit a hijacker to slip through the course of obstacles.'"

SM: "Don't I recall a General Accounting Office issuing a critical report on airport screening?"

DB: "I read that in The Washington Post. The September 2003 article stated that 'the federal government isn't testing the skills of airport security screens as thoroughly as it did before the Sept. 11, 2001 terrorist attacks and needs to develop a recurring training program. But, to be fair, there are times when security people do their job right.'"

SM: "What was that?"

DB: "A family had been vacationing in Orlando, Florida. With their luggage piled up waiting for transportation to the airport, a young girl walked up to them and said she had been given a stuffed teddy bear but that she could not keep it. She handed it to the family's child. The family, in a hurry, accepted it. At the airport, the child had to place the teddy bear on the conveyor belt. Suddenly, the alarm went off. One of the officers looked in amazement at his screen where he could clearly see a .22-caliber gun sewn inside the bear. On being questioned, the parents relayed the story of the 'gift.' They were cleared. While finding a weapon is not unusual, this was considered out of the ordinary. And, this happened despite constant warnings from security personnel that passengers never should accept anything from a stranger."

SM: "I apologize, but again, I have other commitments. However, I want to continue our interview, extended as it has become. Next time, I would like to talk about why hijackers hijack."

DB: "I want to be as helpful as I can, regardless of the time involved."

CHAPTER TWENTY TWO —
MIDEAST TERRORIST MOTIVATION

S M: "I did not realize there were so many sides to this hijacking and terrorism issue. I did get a chance to read your book, and I am intrigued about the chapter on hijacker motivations."

DB: " I wish Dr. Dailey were here to talk about that aspect. But, he has sent me a lot of material, and we have talked at length when I visited him down in Culpeper, Virginia."

SM: "Give it a try, anyhow. I sense this could be an important key."

DB: "We have to separate motivations of past hijackings headed mostly to Cuba from the one horrific devastation of 9/11. That is why Dr. Dailey insisted that his profile, and even the magnetometer, needed to be flexible enough to adjust to the times."

SM: "Let's use that as a starting point."

DB: "As Dr. Dailey noted in the previous book, the first officially reported aircraft hijacking attempt took place on February 21, 1930 in Peru. The first U.S. aircraft hijacking took place on May 1, 1961 aboard a flight from Miami to Key West, Florida. In between those incidents, and then later up until the Task Force came into being, the majority of the hijackings were politically motivated. A few others were for criminal reasons, especially the one involving the infamous Dan (alias D.B.) Cooper. On Thanksgiving eve of 1971 - remember that was more than a year after the Task Force had been disbanded - a passenger by that name boarded a Northwest Orient B-727 in

Portland, Oregon. The plane had hardly gained altitude when he sent a note to the captain that he had a bomb and threatened to blow up the aircraft unless he was given $200,000 and four parachutes. The plane was diverted to the Seattle-Tacoma Airport. His demands were met, and the plane took off for what he said was his destination - Mexico."

SM: "Now I remember the case. Didn't he parachute out of the plane and never was found?"

DB: "Correct. He bailed out somewhere over the state of Washington. His body never was located, and stories abounded. Some say he died; some say he disappeared into the wilderness. There even was a movie made of the incident."

SM: "Well, at least he was not headed to Cuba."

DB: "Who knows what was on his mind? But, the important point is this. Even if the Portland Airport had a security system, my guess is that Cooper would not have been stopped. Although we went to nine airports during our testing phase, Portland was not one of them. Who in the world ever would think a hijacker would do his deed in the northwest United States? An airport in that part of the country, or even in a small town anywhere, would not have the security diligence as, say, La Guardia, or Miami, or even Boston."

SM: " Are you saying trying to cover every airport in the U.S. is hopeless?"

DB: "What I am saying is that some airports are more lax than others. Besides, if all Cooper had was nerve, but not a bomb, he would have passed through easily. Many police departments are not willing to have victims give in to extortion, which is what this was. But, someone made the decision not to take a chance, and paid his demand."

SM: "Maybe he was not even questioned because that new Office at the FAA was not up and running yet to alert all airports."

DB: "An excellent point, although a year and a half had passed between when that Office took over for us, and Cooper got away with his bluff."

SM: "Okay. Let's get back to general motivations."

DB: "In the previous book, Dr. Dailey analyzed earlier worldwide hijackings and concluded that hijackers were a combination of what he called 'homesick Cubans, mentally ill, political terrorists, and even felons.' In his own book, *The Pioneer Heritage,* Dr. Dailey stated that hijackers want attention. 'The gratification apparently comes from an act of high drama representing one brief moment of power and glory in a lifetime of failure,' he wrote. That was a psychological analysis."

SM: "Could there also have been a psychiatric analysis also?"

DB: "You must have read a book titled *The Skyjacker* by Dallas psychiatrist David G. Hubbard published in 1971. I want to discuss him later. After interviewing 20 hijackers, Dr. Hubbard concluded they were 'effeminate, sexually inadequate, ineffectual, generally apolitical individuals who have skyjacked in situations of total personal failure.' He also interjected the possibility that hijackers were subjected to unusual gravity forces. His final conclusions were that hijackings could be controlled by an 'agreement for automatic repatriation,' by his medical research dealing with 'sexual inadequacy' of the hijacker, by adding women to the space program to diminish the notion that flight is 'a male prerogative,' elimination of the death penalty or long prison terms for captured hijackers, and conducting further research."

SM: "Sounds sort of like pie in the sky, if you forgive my own pun."

DB: "That's a good one. But, keep in mind that not one of his conclusions could be adapted to the same kind of airline passenger screening procedure as we produced. This was the same man who wanted Task Force members incarcerated at a mental institution because, as I recall, he felt we were 'nuts' trying to create a psychological profile."

SM: "Well, it's obvious what the motivations of the 9/11 terrorists were."

DB: "I only can give you my views. I am not a psychiatrist, nor a psychologist"

SM: "I'll accept that caveat.

DB: "Terrorism is nothing new. History is replete with various forms of terrorism, sometimes called barbarism. I looked up the definition of terror in the dictionary, and it was enlightening. For example, terror is defined as 'a state of intense fear; a frightening aspect; a cause of anxiety; an appalling thing.' But, the next definition is interesting: 'violent or destructive acts (as bombing) committed by groups in order to intimidate population or government into granting their demands.'"

SM: "Why did you find those last words interesting, as you put it?"

DB: "I think we all may have forgotten that the terrorists did have demands. They wanted the U.S. out of the Middle East, if nothing else. That gets back to my point about understanding the terrorist mind set. We tend to deal with other people around the world as if they were just like us. Terrorists are not like us by any stretch of the imagination. When Dr. Dailey created his profile, he did not presuppose the behavior of hijackers. But, once he did his research, then he had a behavior pattern. By the way, too many people interpret behavior as how people look and talk. That is so misguided. Behavior is a very complicated science, from what I have read. So, developing a behavior pattern only is as realistic as its testing. And, that is the basic fault Dr. Dailey and I find in current procedures."

SM: "Spell that out, please."

DB: "Since 9/11, decision makers have sped headlong into procedures without having done any research. The simplistic 'solution' to protecting us from another 9/11 was to search every passenger. Probably the most important conclusion our testing reached was that you can focus the major part of your anti-hijacking efforts on a manageable number of 'suspects.'"

SM: "Are you implying that since 9/11 the government should have focused on only 2 percent of the flying public?"

DB: "Mideast terrorists are not different from terrorists anywhere in the world. They have total disregard for their lives. They are tenacious in accomplishing their goals. A USA Today article in August 2003 contained two sentences that bear this out: 'Unlike many criminal networks, al-Qaeda seems to learn from its mistakes. Some FBI officials believe the group identified flaws in the 1993 Trade Center garage bombing that killed six people, and then developed a more effective attack. What did they need? The ability to fly? They got that in flight training here. Money? They got that coming in from overseas. They spoke enough English to be able to rent cars and apartments. And they had the discipline to stay out of trouble. Investigators say they have no evidence the hijackers told anyone about their plot.'"

SM: "I know you have protected yourself by saying you are not expert in motivation. But; what is your take on all of this?"

DB: "Willingness of an enemy to die is not new. The Japanese for a long time during World War II would rather die than be captured. The Chinese in the Korean conflict were not afraid to conduct virtual suicide attacks on our troops. And, Vietnam was replete with stories of similar attacks. Then, we come to Iraq, and suddenly we seem to be surprised that an enemy is willing to die if he/she can take victims, whether military or civilian. I put that in the class of underestimating the enemy. The French certainly underestimated the Vietnamese rebels until they suffered a disaster at Dien Bien Phu that forced them to pull out. The Russians underestimated the Afghan rebels until they were forced to pull out. My point is that if you underestimate the enemy, you don't know how to deal with the enemy. I believe we underestimated, or even misunderstood, Mideast terrorism, or believed it would not spread here."

CHAPTER TWENTY THREE

WARNING FLAGS WERE IGNORED

SM: "How could we have known it would spread here and create 9/11?"

DB: "There actually were so many clues over the years that it staggers the mind. Let me start with an op ed piece in the March 27, 2004 issue of The New York Times by Peter R. Neumann. He is identified as a research fellow in international terrorism at the Department of War Studies, King's College, London. The last paragraph really sets the stage for my views: 'In the end, the 9/11 hearings are likely to find that intelligence failure that led to the horrific attacks stemmed from the longstanding problems of wrongly placed agents, failed communications between government departments and lack of resources. But it was also a failure of vision - one for which the current administration must take responsibility.'"

SM: "What's wrong with that conclusion? Sounds pretty lucid to me."

DB: "What's wrong are wrong conclusions. The blame placed on the current administration is wrong. At the risk of sounding like a parrot, the blame goes all the way back to August 1970 when the FAA disbanded the Task Force. You don't have to only blame intelligence and communication dysfunctions, although there were many. Lack of resources? We had the right resource from the get-go - Dr. Dailey's tested and verified profile. All else should have stemmed from that. But, what happened instead? The Nixon administration panicked and ordered all airline passengers to be searched. In hindsight, this eventually played right into the hands of the current terrorists, because for the next three decades efforts to curtail hijackings were not focused on terrorism-related events. Screening yoyoed. There was no continuity because, as I said before, the link was broken because our warnings were ignored."

SM: "I assume you are referring to what was in the Task Force Final Report."

DB: "Exactly! What could be more clear than our use of the term **terrorists** way back in 1978? That is the real shame of 9/11 - totally ignoring what the Task Force concluded *could happen! Had that not been ignored, all the warning signs during the next more than two decades* would *have certainly alerted our decision makers!* If nothing else, and I repeat, *if* nothing else, the February 26, 1993 bombing of the World Trade Center should have set off every security seismograph in this country! I guess it was not important that only six people were killed, and more than 1,000 wounded. Perhaps this was because the bombing happened on the ground. You wouldn't have had to be a terrorism expert to connect the 1978 warnings with the 1993 incident."

SM: "Let me cut right to the chase. So, whom do you blame?"

DB: "I place the crucial blame on the FAA, but collateral blame on each administration from President Nixon through Presidents Ford, Carter, Reagan, the elder Bush, and Clinton, right up to the current Bush. Had the FAA alerted each administration, I feel history would have been very different today. To remind you, I said there were two vital mistakes - the first one that disbanded the Task Force and did not take advantage of its work, and 'Black September' which took away the focus on Dr. Dailey's profile as Step One of a viable screening procedure. And, I do not need to go into the tepid approach the FAA took to plenty of warning signs. When the FAA issued three information circulars to airports in 1998 of a possible terrorist hijacking along the East Coast, I cannot find any evidence that the agency brought back a modified profile as Step One. According to a Boston Globe story of May 26, 2002, 'Bush administration and FAA officials have characterized the pre-September intelligence as too broad to defend against and said they lacked a credible hijacking threat.'"

SM: "Don't you think that under the circumstances the administration did all it could?"

DB: "No. To me, it was more of the same - keep on screening all passengers with primary reliance on the magnetometer, followed by making too many innocent people suspects. From all the information I have been able to glean, the profile could well have identified all 19 terrorists as 'suspects' because they fit enough of the profile to be detained. The fact that they somehow smuggled those box cutters on the flights is a secondary matter. What good would those weapons have been if those flights had taken off without the terrorists? The fact that some of the terrorists had faulty passports also is a secondary matter. I have to keep harping away at the assertion that 'suspects' had to raise more than just one warning flag."

SM: "Can you say that our administrations and the FAA were not aware of international incidents?"

DB: "I am sure they were. But, I must remind you that our Task Force had an excellent representative from the Office of International Aviation Affairs, Lee Jett. Dr. Reighard, our chairman, knew full well there had to be international implications. And, we did coordinate with the International Civil Aviation Organization (ICAO). If memory serves me correctly, we hoped that what we did would be a model for nations around the world. What good does it do for us to have security measures when foreign airports have different measures? We are getting into the field of geopolitics, and notice the Task Force did not have anyone representing that discipline. We wanted to stay outside of politics. Very few members of Congress really were interested in our work, or their staff members surely would have alerted those lawmakers about an impending crisis."

SM: "Let's bring the situation up to date. Won't you agree that a lot has been done to upgrade the screening process?"

CHAPTER TWENTY FOUR —
BUREAUCRACY BUMBLING

DB: "This really opens up a can of worms. At the outset, I will not deny my bias about this aspect."

SM: "Why do you take such a hard line?"

DB: "I must confess that Dr. Dailey and I virtually cried after 9/11 because we believed that had the work the Task Force did still been Step One, the catastrophe could have been prevented. But, we were trumped by bureaucracy. And, I believe I have covered that subject through your questions. And, look at the bureaucratic consequences of 9/11. We have a continuing military struggle in two Mideast countries. We have continuous rising numbers of casualties. We continue to pour billions of dollars into this effort. And, now we have yet another layer of bureaucracy - the Department of Homeland Security and all its subdivisions."

SM: "Let's pursue that aspect in more detail."

DB: "To do that, I want to cite an article in the March 11, 2003 issue of The New York Times, because it goes to the heart of this matter. Interestingly enough, this appeared in the business travel section."

SM: "Did you say business travel?"

DB: "Yes. I thought the columnist Joe Sharkey did a good job, but inadvertently identified the core of what is wrong. The column started off describing the first electronic background system called 'CAPPS I.' That stood for 'Computer Assisted Passenger Prescreening System.'

It was put into service in the later 1990's and adjusted after 9/11. In February 2003, the system was upgrade to 'CAPPS II.' As Sharkey explained it, the original system 'was designed to select passengers for extra security screening based on a number of undisclosed indicator criteria.' Sound familiar?"

SM: "I just know you're going to tell me that is Dr. Dailey's profile."

DB: "Sharkey then notes that 'CAPPS II has been partly designed to address the faults inherent in the original program, which has been at the heart of the much-discussed airport security hassle complaint that airlines blame for at least part of their drop in business travel revenue.' Sound familiar?"

SM: "Hmmm. Oh, yes. The Task Force made a point of developing a system that would not adversely affect airline revenue."

DB: "Good, so far. Sharkey goes on to describe a 'new computer-based system (that) will evaluate precise personal information about a passenger booking a ticket, and then assign that passenger one of three color-based security ratings.'"

SM: "Oh, yes - green for no problem, yellow for additional screening, and red for hold the phone you're in trouble."

DB: "It seems, according to the column, that privacy groups did not think much of 'CAPPS II.' And, they took it out on Delta Air Lines, which had volunteered to test the new program."

SM: "I'm with you so far, but I don't have a clue where you are going with this."

DB: "Both 'CAPPS' programs gathered information about Americans traveling on American planes, by and large."

SM: "So, what's wrong with that?"

DB: "But, *we are supposed to be looking for Mideast terrorists who might want to repeat 9/11. Instead, we are looking at innocent American travelers.*"

SM: "Maybe we were thinking those terrorists might have more of their kinds of people who are Americans."

DB: "If that were the case, then there should have been multiple 'CAPPS' systems - one to look for hardened Mideast terrorists, and another for Mideast terrorist 'moles.' Some of the original profile elements certainly can be included, others can be omitted, and new ones can be added."

SM: "Why haven't you and Dr. Dailey made your suggestions known to the right people?"

DB: "Lord knows, we have tried. We contacted the White House, Members of Congress, the Secretary of Homeland Security, the Administrator of the TSA, the Secretary of Transportation, the Administrator of the FAA, and members of both the electronic and print media. We have a perfect score - not one of those were interested. That is why this book is the last alternative."

SM: "Aren't you being provocative just to get attention?"

DB: "Whatever is provocative, to use your term, is based on fact, or personal observation based on my experience and background."

SM: "Aren't the 'CAPPS' systems a good way to spot potential Mideast terrorist hijackers?"

DB: "The Council on Foreign Relations issued a Q&A sheet on terrorism in 2003. One of the questions was, 'Do suicide terrorists fit a common profile?' The answer was: 'Experts used to think so, but after September 11, they are less sure. As Brian Jenkins of the RAND think tank has put it, typical Middle Eastern suicide bombers were usually thought to be poor, not very well educated, and possibly psychologically damaged young men in their early 20's. Experts used to argue that men who were older, better educated, and had more social status, would be less inclined to kill themselves. This would normally have been a good bet, but the September 11 attackers were older - particularly those who clearly knew it was to be a suicide mission. They had better educations and appear to have been far more sophisticated than their predecessors. The profile of suicide attackers now requires revision.'"

SM: "That is an interesting answer."

DB: "Here's another one. Question: 'Can suicide terrorism be prevented?' Answer: 'Experts say that if a competent terrorist organization can operate freely and keep its operations secret, stopping its suicide attacks may be extremely difficult.'"

SM: "It sounds more and more like we don't have a chance of preventing suicide attacks in this country."

DB: "As critical as I have sounded of the bureaucracy, I also am an optimist. If bureaucrats can be flexible, if they will reread our Final Report, and if they understand the approach we took with Dr. Dailey's profile, I firmly believe we can do the best we can. No, we cannot stop all attempts. We said that more than 30 years ago. But, at least we can do better. However, as I said before, suicide terrorism has to be dealt with at its origin, and that is beyond what we are talking about here. According to my military experience, and I am not a member of the Joints Chiefs of Staff by any means, you do not want to fight a war of attrition. That gives terrorists the advantage. They even can go underground for a while, and resurface when they feel the time is right. Fighting terrorism on rigid bureaucratic terms is a lesson in futility."

SM: "Let's continue to focus on the present with an eye toward the future."

CHAPTER TWENTY FIVE —
PRESENT TENSED-UP SITUATION

DB: "Remember that spate of airline cancellations in early 2004 because of terrorists scares? That is just what we wanted to avoid by having the upper hand in publicizing our efforts. And, that is why I claim one of the aims of terrorists is to hit us in the financial belly. Airlines depend a lot on business clients, and during early 2004 those clients decided not to fly as often."

SM: "But, hasn't that been turned around?"

DB: "Thank goodness, yes. Dysfunctional as screening is, it still presents an added obstacle to hijacking attempts. However, I have another view of this. I believe that Mideast terrorists now are concentrating on a guerilla war in Iraq and Afghanistan. That is using much of the terrorists' resources, not only in money but in lives. Besides, the 9/11 effort took a lot of time and planning."

SM: "I don't think I heard that take on terrorism before."

DB: "Again, I am not an expert in such matters, but I continue to look at things from what I think is the terrorist point of view. They have an agenda that can change with the wind. That is not to say we can afford to let our guard down. Quite the contrary. But, that begs the question of what is the most effective deterrent. I do not believe there is one particular deterrent. But, there is a lot that can be done. For example, sharing information seems all to simple an answer for what was a war of fiefdoms for many years regarding terrorism. At the risk of repeating myself, you have to understand the bureaucracy and its motto of protecting turf at all costs. Even within agencies you can find bureaucratic jealousies. When I worked at the Department of Justice, Attorney General Ramsey Clark was J. Edgar Hoover's boss. Maybe he was, on paper, but Hoover was his own boss of the FBI. I learned quickly that trying to get cooperation from the FBI was an exercise in patience."

SM: "I think we all know about Hoover and the FBI."

DB: "There continues to be controversy over how to react to tension. I saw on television that officials cannot figure out how to enforce the no-fly zone over the nation's capital. It seems there is not one central figure coordinating how to deal with private planes that enter that zone. It seems that at least on 350 occasions, military aircraft were 'scrambled' to escort those errant planes.

SM: "I guess we're entering the realm of sharing information."

DB: "That surely is a hot button topic. Zillions of words already have been spoken about the lack of same among intelligence gathering organizations. Currently, efforts have been centered around databases. The Terrorist Screening Center, run by the FBI, coordinates information throughout the government and even throughout industry. But, I have to keep repeating, that while such information about potential terrorism acts is useful, it translates into searching innocent Americans."

SM: "Are you implying this is useless?"

DB: "What I am implying is that such information would be useful if from it a credible screening system for **potential Mideast terrorists** can be developed. I know I am repeating myself, but there has to be two separate screening systems."

SM: "I seem to recall the Clinton administration allocated $300 million for counter-terror measures, better screening of airline passengers, more FBI agents to deal with airport security, and more bomb-sniffing animals."

DB: "That was the White House Commission on Aviation Safety

and Security which Vice President Gore chaired. That group came into being following the July 1996 explosion of TWA Flight 800 over Long Island Sound. President Clinton signed the allocation into law in October."

SM: "How can you not say that the government has been trying to do what it can to prevent a repeat of 9/11 ?"

DB: "That's a fair question. Government is doing a lot. But, Dr. Dailey and I maintain it is focused in the wrong direction. A story from WorldNetDaily in March 2002 asserted: 'A computerized system used by airlines to screen suspicious passengers failed to expose the 19 Arab hijackers on Sept. 11 because it omits key terrorist-profiling indicators such as national origin, a Federal Aviation Administration security official says. If airlines had profiled passengers based on human criteria, he says, the roughly 3,000 Americans who died that day might still be alive. If human-profiling was conduced on the terrorists who were made selectees that day, then maybe some or the entire plot could have been avoided.' The official was not named, only identified as working in the agency's Aviation Security Division. The system he referred to that CAPPS II. The official went on to say, 'CAPPS was developed because the airline industry didn't want to do human-profiling. Yet human-profiling is the single-biggest deterrent against terrorism in the aviation industry.' Pretty strong words, wouldn't you say?"

SM: "Can you assure me he is not one of your plants?"

DB: "In all honesty, I had never heard of the guy, and never knew his views until I got that story off the Internet"

SM: "Isn't there a concern over sharing information about passengers?"

DB: "The Washington Post in September 2003 reported the airline JetBlue admitting 'it violated its own privacy policy by supplying names, phone numbers and addresses of one million passengers to an Alabama company called Torch Concepts, which was working on an Army database to identify suspected terrorists. This has been a concern of civil libertarians for some time.'"

SM: "Don't I recall something about airlines being ordered to share such information?"

DB: "You're probably referring to another Post story three days later stating that TSA Administrator James A. Loy threatened 'to compel U.S. airlines to cooperate in handing over data about their passengers for a new government computer screening system, which has been widely criticized as violating privacy rights.' Loy was referring to CAPPS II. It never happened."

SM: "Then, there were those color codes."

DB: "Oh, yes. If you had a green card (a terrible pun), you aced the boarding process. If you got yellow, you got some extra interrogation. If you got red, you not only could not board the flight, but in all probability you had to face the law. Me, I'm red-green color blind. Seriously, this was just grasping at straws."

SM: "By the way, what did you think about that order that prevented you from going to the airplane restroom for 30 minutes after takeoff and 30 minutes prior to landing?"

DB: "Thank goodness that finally got rescinded. Forgive me, but that pissed me off. I had prostate cancer surgery some years ago, and that decreased the size of my bladder. I never know when I have to make a beeline for the john. And, I am sure there are others with worse problems than mine."

SM: "I think this is a good time for us to stop. I have some commitments for the next two days, so let's get together right after that"

DB: "See you then."

CHAPTER TWENTY SIX —
INTERNATIONAL IMPLICATIONS

SM: "There seems to be one area we barely touched on, and that is how other nations around the world deal with terrorism and hijackings."

DB: "I must confess all I know about this is what I read in the papers and hear and see on television. But, having been to Europe several times on vacation with my wife, I only can tell you about our experiences at various airports. I don't recall any of the major airports overseas requiring passengers to take off their shoes, or to have a lot of strip searches as we do here. That is not to say other nations do not take airport security seriously. On the contrary. We found that places like Heathrow in England and DeGaulle in France are thorough but fair in their security. Amsterdam was more relaxed, as was Helsinki, but still competent. Ironically, each airport has its own levels of what will set off the metal detectors."

SM: "I recall you had said that even in this country, each airline sets its own standards."

DB: " Yes. As I mentioned before, each country does the same. I ran across a December 2002 Internet story issued by BBC News that had some interesting comments. A top security consultant was quoted as saying 'it was essential that (armed) air marshals were backed up by improved security on the ground.'"

SM: "That sounds familiar."

DB: "The point is that virtually every country agrees with the Task

Force's basic premise that the major focus of dealing with potential terrorist hijackers is to keep them from getting on the aircraft in the first place. As that security official observed, 'The key with airline security is a combination of good intelligence and physical security measures, with a heavy emphasis on passenger profiling.'"

SM: "Where have I heard that before?"

DB: "There was one aspect of that story that got my attention. The security official would prefer having former soldiers - with combat and special forces training—to become armed air marshals, but to wear civilian clothing on flights. '(They) would mingle with other passengers before they boarded the plane and look for signs of potential trouble throughout the flight.'"

SM: "What is your concern?"

DB: "If armed marshals are in civilian clothes, the question is whether they would be a better deterrent than if they were in uniform. If in civilian clothes, chances are they only could be carrying sidearms. There also is the issue of how passengers would feel if they saw uniform armed guards on their flight. Some research needs to be done on this. My memory may be faulty on this, but I thought the Israelis used uniformed soldiers on El Al flights. Then, there is yet another issue that is a lot more complicated."

SM: "And, what is that?"

DB: "Suppose an armed guard or two is assigned to a flight from Tel Aviv to New York. Is that guard an Israeli and a U.S. sky marshal? Suppose there is an attempted hijacking within the territorial limit of the United States. Are there legal ramifications if the Israeli guard swings into action? Conversely, suppose the attempted hijacking takes place right after takeoff, and the guard is a U.S. marshal. Does he or she have the legal right to interfere? Do the same issues arise if the flight is from New York to Tel Aviv? Could there be a combination of an Israeli guard and a U.S. sky marshal? There may well be international arrangements for such situations that we do not know about. International treaties are hard to come by as it is. As with the United Nations, there often is more heat than light. International negotiations often end up with what I would describe as toothless agreements."

SM: "You had some observations in your other book about international involvement."

DB: "As I noted, ICAO adopted what became known as the *Tokyo Convention*. All it did was provide for the return of hijacked aircraft to the nation of origin. A year later, ICAO passed the *Hague Convention*. While it called for punishment or extradition of airplane hijackers, the choice was left up o the signers of the pact. That same year, ICAO drafted a *Montreal Convention* that proposed severe penalties for attacks in flight, as well as a treaty under which any nation that protected, did not prosecute, or did not extradite hijackers would face an international boycott. Both efforts fell flatter than a pancake. So, as I said, trying to get international agreement on aircraft hijacking is not an easy thing to accomplish."

SM: "As far as you can recall, was there any agreement on weapons that guards could use?"

DB: "If you remember my recounting that Fort Dix fiasco, there was special ammunition that would not penetrate the skin of the aircraft. But, as I recall, there was some question about whether that ammunition would affect the electrical system. It is important to note that the security consultant I mentioned was quoted as saying that 'firearms would be the very last resort.' To me, that is very good advice, as was his further comment that 'it was unrealistic to expect (armed guards) presence to mean there would be no more hijack attempts. Yes, it will be a deterrent to certain people, but of course there will always be someone who suddenly commits a crazed act during the flight.'"

SM: "It sounds as if international cooperation was lukewarm at best."

DB: "If so, it was not because the Task Force did not try. We worked with our Department of State, as well as with other diplomatic bodies. In June 1970, the Task Force invited 54 nations to attend a briefing of our work, including Dr. Dailey's profile. However, each nation did its own thing. But, as you can tell by 9/11, a lot still remains to be done about international cooperation."

CHAPTER TWENTY SEVEN —
WHAT NEEDS TO BE DONE

SM: "So, where do we go from here?"

DB: "The first step seems hopeless - that is, eradicating Mideast terrorism. Pandora's Box that released the evils of terrorism was not opened only on 9/11. The 9/11 Commission's Final Report lists Mideast terrorist acts after terrorist acts over decades. What bothers me is that we do not seem to have learned many lessons from those acts. It almost seems to we turned a blind eye and a deaf ear to such happenings until they occurred on U.S. soil. But, as pointed out before, Mideast terrorists bombed the World Trade Center in 1993! What more wake-up call did we need, especially at the FAA? Tepid warnings? That was a bureaucratic response, and the agency should accept full blame for that."

SM: "But, the FAA wasn't solely to blame. There were all those intelligence dysfunctions."

DB: "Despite those dysfunctions, I blame the FAA for not wondering whether the 1993 Mideast terrorist act against the World Trade Center could be translated into a Mideast terrorist act against U.S. aircraft. I don't think that should have taken a Mideast terrorism expert to at least consider that possibility. Again, as I have pointed out, our Task Force Final Report clearly warned about the possibility of **terrorist hijackings** against our airplanes. And, that is why I say one of the real mistakes of 9/11 can be traced to the disbanding of the Task Force in 1970."

SM: "Are you saying all we are doing is locking the barn door after the horse has been stolen, as the old saying goes?"

DB: "What I am saying I don't think we are using the right response. After the spate of bombings in the Middle East in late July 2005, we start using random searches. That, to me, is like a doctor prescribing an aspirin for a headache that closer scrutiny would have discovered to be a brain tumor."

SM: "Okay, get specific now. What should we be doing ?"

DB: "I would strongly suggest going back to the approach Dr. Reighard and the Task Force took. That is, develop statistics on the acts of Mideast terrorism - how they occurred, where they occurred, how they were accomplished, et cetera. I suggest the result of that research would conclude that potential Mideast terrorist hijackers are *a fraction of 1 percent of the flying public in the U.S.* Using Dr. Dailey's approach, a list of common characteristics needs to be developed into a profile for those few people. Next, as our traveling team did, those characteristics need to be tested for verification of so few people being involved. If that proves out, then that profile needs to be Step One, not the metal detector. Let's give Mideast terrorists credit for being deadly creative on how to develop 'weapons' to use on specific targets."

SM: "Well, it ought to be easy to spot Mideast terrorists trying to board a flight, shouldn't it?"

DB: "I think you are headed for 'racial' profiling. I doubt such terrorists would look and dress like Mideast people. From what I have read about the spate of bombings, some of the terrorists blended into the surrounding crowd. Remember, under Dr. Dailey's profile, a 'suspect' had to trigger at least half a dozen of the behavioral characteristics. Passenger screening has to be precise to be effective. In late July 2005, a flight was diverted because some passengers became suspicious of three 'Arab-looking' men walking up and down the aisles. It turned out that the three men were innocent businessmen. Had the adjusted profile been Step One, and the men were stopped before boarding, they would have been taken aside and questioned. If they had produced proper identification, and been subjected to a body search, they would have been cleared. The flight crew would have known about this, so that when other passengers because concerned, they could have been assured that the three men were 'kosher.'"

SM: "If I understand the point you are making in this case, that plane never would have been diverted."

DB: "That also goes back to what I said about the need to clear innocent passengers as quickly as possible. That approach was part of the Task Force effort to allay the fears of the major airlines that our search procedure would ruin their business. It is interesting that passenger traffic remains high even though they willingly put up with long security lines. What I am saying is that I don't think the overwhelming majority of air travelers should have to put up with those delays. But, we keep hearing and reading stories of those humiliating body searches."

SM: "Wouldn't we be taking a chance on clearing those passengers, some of whom may be Mideast terrorists in disguise?"

DB: "That was the same concern when our Task Force was in operation. To repeat, we felt there was no way to stop all hijacking attempts, even when most of them would end up in Cuba, and the hijackers were not terrorists. I don't care what system is in effect today - determined Mideast terrorists will give up their lives to accomplish their goal of hijacking an airplane if that is their plan. With all the military might we have in Iraq and Afghanistan, those terrorists still are giving us fits."

SM: "You've spent more time telling me what has gone wrong than what has gone right So, let's get specific on what you feel should be done to stop making screening, as you describe it 'ineffective, inefficient, and humiliating.'"

DB: "Fair enough. **First**, I would ask top decision makers to read the Task Force Final Report, which is FAA Manual AM-78-35, especially the pages I enumerated that contain those dire predictions three decades before they actually happened."

SM: "As I recall, the Manual is available from the National Technical Information Service."

DB: "**Second**, I would ask decision makers to study how Dr. Dailey created his profile through data analysis, how we tested it, why the ACLU approved it, and how a New York Federal Court judge ruled the procedure constitutional. So, I am asking decision makers to use the same epidemiological approach Dr. Dailey did to reach *realistic* conclusions instead of *political* ones. As such, I ask decision makers to adapt Dr. Dailey's profile to present-day circumstances, but to insure such profile be Step One. That would enable *innocent* passengers to be quickly cleared and boarded."

SM: "What would come next?"

DB: "**Third**, I would ask decision makers to understand that this approach not only can save millions and millions of dollars badly needed for domestic programs, but also to making screening *more efficient, more effective, and less humiliating.* That can be done by having one set of screening procedures for *potential Mideast terrorist hijackers* but another set for *potential non-Mideast terrorist hijackers* such as 'disturbed' domestic offenders."

SM: "That's something I have not heard before. Go on, please."

DB: "**Fourth**, I would ask decision makers to work more closely with airline officials to expedite baggage inspections so that the flow to and from aircraft is as smooth and fast as possible within bounds of security. That may include another look at carry-on luggage. During our testing, we worked closely with Eastern Airlines first, and others later, to hear what they had to say. We did not want to put a crimp on airline passenger revenue."

SM: "I am led to believe this is being done, but I understand your concern about trying to improve whatever is being done."

DB: "**Fifth**, I would ask decision makers to develop a positive rapport with the news media. We worked hard at that, often asking trusted reporters how they would treat our efforts. We also tried to anticipate reporters' questions and concerns. We did not want to read, hear, and see stories about how messed up the system was. That is why we were so adamant about testing our procedure not only to determine the effect it would have on passengers, but also to get a feel for how reporters would treat our efforts."

SM: "Are you saying you wanted to control the media?"

DB: "Absolutely not! On the contrary, we wanted to be as open as we could with the media without bounds of security. As I already have explained, we emphasized why we had bounds of security. Of course, the media today are not the media of yesterday. That is why there has to be a new way of dealing with the media. As a former reporter, I role-played with my colleagues to get their reaction. Naturally, there will be those reporters who for whatever motive will not find anything positive to say. And, if you recall, out of some 200 stories I documented during our testing phase when we had news conferences at every airport we used, only half a dozen were negative. You just have to accept that, and as the old Johnny Mercer tune goes, 'Accentuate the positive.'"

SM: I hope you do not plan to sing that song."

DB: "You really do not want to hear me try to sing. **Sixth**, I would hope decision makers would read other books on earlier events, such as Jim Arey's *The Skyjackers*."

SM: "You're asking a lot, especially relating this to current terrorism activities."

DB: "Well, look how security officials still are trying to come to grips with screening methods. The Associated Press reported in mid-April 2005 that according to 'a House member who has been briefed on the contents' that '(t)wo upcoming government reports will say the quality of screening at airports is no better now than before the Sept. 11 attacks.'"

SM: "Any more suggestions?"

DB: "One last one. **Seventh**, I hope decision makers develop an apolitical understanding not only of what motivates Mideast terrorists, but also how any Mideast terrorist hijacking provides a floor plan of how we can create and test the proper procedures to deal with that. Assuming that all domestic passengers are *potential Mideast terrorist hijackers is* the *wrong approach.*"

SM: "What makes you think you have the answers?"

DB: "I'm not offended by that question at all. Neither Dr. Dailey nor I pretend to have all the answers. What we are saying is that present day procedures do not have a sound basis or premise. It almost is like tossing darts at a procedure board in front of you, and wherever they land, that is the procedure *de jour*. Random searches in this scheme of things are unrealistic because they are. nothing more than knee-jerk reactions just for the sake of reactions. The very nature of uncertainty prevails today. What amazes me is that passengers are willing to put up with delays and humiliation because why consider political brainwashing when there are more efficient, effective, and less humiliating ways to accomplish security."

SM: "Is there anything we have not covered that you would like to bring up?"

DB: "If you can spare the time, you might be interested in the relationship between Dr. Dailey's profile and my endless battle with The New York Times on who deserves the credit for the only psychological profile used to screen passengers."

SM: "You've got my attention on that one."

CHAPTER TWENTY EIGHT

THESE ARE THE (NEW YORK) TIMES THAT TRY A MAN'S PROFESSIONAL SOUL

DB: "On January 16, 2005, The Times Sunday Magazine ran an article titled *The First Hijackers - Re-Evaluation* by Andreas Killen. The article did not identify the author, nor present any credentials to justify writing such an article. In recounting a number of pre-9/11 hijackers, Killen cited 'an influential study, *The Skyjacker*, by David Hubbard (who) enumerated common passengers' responses to hijackings. Hubbard, a psychiatrist, was hired by the F.A.A. to create the psychological profile used for screening passengers.'"

SM: "Just a minute. All along you have been telling me that it was Dr. Dailey who did that."

DB: "Of course. The minute I saw those words, I fired off an e-mail letter-to-the-editor. I challenged the allegation that Hubbard had some such a profile, since I was on the Task Force from beginning to end. I cited the Manual and my own previous book, *NINE/ELEVEN*, which detailed the work of our group to show that only Dr. Dailey's profile was *the* (meaning only) profile 'used for screening passengers." I also cited the ACLU approval and the New York Federal Court case. About a week later, I received a call from a Sarah H. Smith, a fact checker. In essence, she said her staff had 'evidence' to support the reference to Hubbard. By the way, I said I found it interesting that (1) the article did not properly refer to him as Dr. Hubbard

- a psychiatrist being a medical doctor, and (2) questioning **why a psychiatrist** would produce a **psychological profile.** She would not back down. On January 25, I e-mailed her stating that I checked with a former FAA colleague who did some later work for the Task Force, and he said he never heard of Dr. Hubbard. Checking with Dr. Dailey, he agreed that Dr. Hubbard was one of some 200 people who submitted ideas to deal with the then hijackings, mostly to Cuba."

SM: "What was his suggestion?"

DB: "As John and I best recall, he wanted prostitutes put aboard flights to entice hijackers because he felt hijackers had sexual problems."

SM: "You're putting me on."

DB: "In all honesty, that is our recollection. Anyhow, I followed that e-mail up the next day wanting to see her 'evidence.' I said I had searched the Internet and could not find any reference to Dr. Hubbard except that he wrote that book. I suggested she read the Task Force Final Report as well as the New York Federal Court decision where John's profile was specifically cited. I also noted that the FAA gave John its highest cash award at the time, $3,000, for his profile work. Two days later, I sent her another e-mail stating that I just bought Dr. Hubbard's book, and read it carefully from front to back. I stated, 'NOWHERE IN ALL 262 PAGES WILL YOU FIND ONE MENTION - JUST ONE MENTION - OF ANYTHING TO BACK UP WHAT YOU BELIEVE IS THE FACT THAT HE WAS HIRED BY THE FAA TO CREATE A PSYCHOLOGICAL PROFILE USED FOR PASSENGER SCREENING.' I'd like to talk more about his book later. I mentioned that during my reporter days, I handled letters to the editor."

SM: "That must have gotten her attention."

DB: "Indeed it did. On February 8, she e-mailed me with this long one-paragraph response: 'I was surprised to get your letter of 2/6/05. (I have not recounted every e-mail I sent, but she cited eight of them.) It takes time to determine whether a correction is warranted in a case like this, where there seems to be evidence supporting both sides.. I am grateful for our continuing patience and hope that you will understand that I have not dismissed your concerns, but am addressing them with the same care with which I respond to all our correspondents.'"

SM: "Sounds reasonable to me."

DB: "I suppose I should have been flattered by being called a correspondent. Anyhow, she also said she never received a copy of my book that I had sent. So, I mailed a second one with a return card. She never acknowledged receiving it, but the Post Office assured me it got to The Times. Be that as it may, I sent another e-mail that same day saying that 'I would appreciate a look at what you describe as evidence supporting the claim that Dr. Hubbard was the one hired by the FAA to develop a psychological profile used to screen passengers.' I also stated I had surfed Google looking for such evidence, but could not find any. I added that 'this issue has gone on for a month. For the final time, I ask that you let me know exactly what evidence you and/or your staff have found to support Dr. Hubbard's claim.'"

SM: "You seem to be getting nowhere slowly."

DB: I do not give up easily. On February 20, I sent yet another e-mail arguing, 'I cannot fathom why you deign to protect the article's author when you cannot provide me with supporting material.' I sent copies to The Times Executive Editor Bill Keller and to Public Editor (the ombudsman) Dan Okrent."

SM: "That should have gotten someone's attention."

DB: "Yes."

SM: " Well, finally.'"

DB: "An aide to the Public Editor e-mailed me saying he could not find any 'record of any correspondence between you and this office going back three months. Please forward any previous correspondence between us so that I may raise the issue with the appropriate editors.'

I responded with a long e-mail recounting the correspondence. The following day, the Public Editor himself e-mailed me saying, 'I haven't dropped this yet. I should be able to get back to you with something definitive in a matter of days."

SM: "Hope springs eternal."

DB: "I was naive to hope so. But, I did find it odd that on the previous day, his aide said he could not find any correspondence from me, but within 24 hours his boss clearly intimated that he had been looking into the matter. The Public Editor sent another e-mail later that day stating, 'I have begun to look into your concern. We usually tell readers that this process may take up to two weeks. We will certainly try to expedite this but I cannot guarantee you of an immediate response.' He also said I should send e-mails directly to him because copies are not considered. To me, an e-mail is an e-mail whether it is sent directly, or is a copy. The following day, the aide got back into the act stating, 'We ask readers not to cc. us on this they want us to respond to because we get spammed and needlessly cc'd on letters which have nothing to do with this office and while we review these messages the volume of messages we receive force us to focus our full attention on messages sent directly to us.'"

SM: "Well, that cleared things up."

DB: "You josh. On March 16, I noted that the following day 'marks two months since I challenged this story.' And still no answers to my challenges. So much for rapid response. I sent yet another e-mail reminder on March 30, which did prompt a response from the Public Editor. He stated, 'I have advised the editors of the magazine that it would appear to be inaccurate to say that Dr. Hubbard was commissioned to do a profile.'"

SM: "Your patience was finally rewarded."

DB: "Not so fast. The next sentence noted that 'a correction might be phrased to indicate that he was not commissioned to do the profile, but was one of several consulted on the subject.'"

SM: "I'm not sure what to make of that."

DB: "What I made of it was a typical bureaucratic 'spin.' I worked in the government for 24 years, and I know a 'spin' when I see one. Of course, now I really wanted the evidence to prove Dr. Hubbard even was a consultant But, the Public Editor beat me to the punch."

SM: "I think I need an aspirin at this point."

DB: "He went on to say, 'However, they (the editors) point out that they have no independent proof that he was not commissioned to do a profile, and that a correction without such proof might in turn be inaccurate.'"

SM: "Come again?"

DB: "On the one hand, he admitted there was no proof that Dr. Hubbard did what the article claimed he did, but on the other, there was no proof that Dr. Hubbard was not hired to do it. The Public Editor continued, 'Given how far in the past these events took place such proof may not be available. However, if you could provide authoritative assertion from someone without a vested interest in discrediting Dr. Hubbard, I would of course become more insistent about a correction. I'm not suggesting that you aren't being truthful with me - only that you yourself may not have access to all the available information.'"

SM: "What was your response to that?"

DB: "If I were a Times fact-checker, I would have contacted the FAA. If Dr. Hubbard had been hired as a consultant, there had to be some record of his work, if nothing else to justify whatever money he would have been paid. But, I resisted the urge to insult The Times by telling the paper how to do some solid and basic investigating."

SM: "Was that the end of it?"

DB: "Not by a long shot. The Public Editor e-mailed me wanting me to ask Dr. Dailey to tell him what Dr. Hubbard's role was. First of all, I gave Okrent John's phone number, feeling it was up to him to make the call, not get me involved as a third party. Second, I already had e-mailed The Tunes what John had confirmed with me. What more could I do? So, once again, I asked to see the so-called 'evidence' that Dr. Hubbard did what the article claimed he had done."

SM: "What did Dr. Dailey say?"

DB: "I called John several days later. He said he never received the call. But then, I saw an article in The Times that Okrent was ending his contract as Public Editor at the end of April, and that Byron Calame would replace him. But, I had one more go with Okrent. On April 21, I e-mailed him noting that a Los Angeles Times reporter was fired for not being able to verify the courses of some quotations he used. I compared that lack of verification with the case here. As you phrased it early, I got nowhere slowly. That means, no response from Okrent."

SM: "Why didn't you just give up at this point?"

DB: "No me. I then wrote a letter on May 5 to Times Publisher Arthur Ochs Sulzberger, Jr., recounting my frustration."

SM: "Did he respond?"

DB: "The response came from Allan M. Siegel, assistant managing editor and the 'standards editor' of The Times. I never knew such a title existed. In a May 11 letter, Siegel sent me a copy of the correction that appeared in the May 8 issue of the Sunday Magazine. I had missed it."

SM: "You finally won the battle, to my surprise."

DB: "If only that were true."

SM: "Run that by me again?"

DB: "The correction read: 'An article on Jan. 16, about aircraft hijackings in the 1970's, referred imprecisely to the role played by a psychiatrist, Dr. **David Hubbard** (yes, bold letters), in the creation of a psychological profile of potential hijackers for the F.A.A. Dr. Hubbard did develop such a profile, used by both the government and industry. But an F.A.A. task force in operation from 1969 to 1971 developed an earlier profile of potential hijackers, relying on the work of one of its members, John T. Dailey. This omission was brought to the attention of the editors shortly after the article appeared, and this correction was delayed for further research.'"

SM: "So, that ended the matter."

DB: "Hardly. First of all, Dr. Hubbard, a psychiatrist, would not be doing a psychological profile. The two professions may have some common ground, but a psychiatrist has to be a medical doctor; a psychologist does not. Second, the correction reiterated that Dr. Hubbard 'did develop such a profile,' still without providing any proof. Third, the Task Force ended its work in 1970, not 1971. That is sloppy journalism. Fourth, while the correction did use the title Dr. for Hubbard, it did not do the same for Dailey, who has a doctorate. That too is sloppy journalism. And, fifth, the correction kept referring to 'potential' hijackers. They all were actual hijackers. Even sloppier journalism. But, the kicker was Siegel's accompanying letter."

SM: "What did it say?"

DB: "One sentence tells it all: 'Quite honestly I cannot imagine what further research would have taken us nearly four months to carry out, but I hope all's well that ends well.'"

SM: "What do I get the feeling that this did not end things well?"

DB: "A new chapter was about to unfold. I suddenly received a phone call from someone who only identified himself as Bill Borders of The Times. He said he was conducting an impartial inquiry into the matter. We went over the entire matter, and he said he would call back. When he did, he said he concluded The Times did all it could, and nothing more could be done."

SM: "Another anticlimax? What more could be done?"

DB: "I e-mailed Borders, who never told me what position he held, offering the following proposed correction: 'A May 8 correction referring to a January 16 New York Times Sunday Magazine article about aircraft hijackings needs further clarification. While the article stated that Dr. David Hubbard, a psychiatrist, 'created the psychological profile used for screening passengers,' further research has concluded that the only (such) profile was created by Dr. John T. Dailey, a member of the agency's Task Force on Deterrence of Air Piracy and the FAA's chief psychologist. His profile was tested during 1969-70. While Dr. Hubbard in his book *The Skyjacker* established a psychiatric profile of hijackers, there is no evidence that he was hired by the FAA to apply his conclusions to a passenger screening procedure.'"

SM: "And, when did that appear?"

DB: "You jest. Nothing ever appeared."

SM: "What was your next move?"

DB: "I e-mailed the new Public Editor. On June 8, he responded: 'I consider the Dailey-Hubbard dispute over credit for profiling a question that has been dealt with appropriately by Allan M. Siegel. I have plenty to do in dealing with new issues, so I don't envision revisiting the Dailey-Hubbard question.'"

SM: "I guess that put you in your place."

DB: "Pretty much. I tried several more times to plead my case, but Siegel ended it all in a July 5 letter: 'I don't know what else we can do to satisfy you that The Times has considered your position repeatedly and as objectively as we know how. I sent out your position fully in a letter to you on June 16, which also cited earlier conversations between you and William Borders. I am sorry that I cannot think of any further recourse we can properly accord you.'"

SM: "End of your journalistic journey."

DB: "Yes, from that perspective. But, then comes a piece by Op-Ed Editor David Shipley in the July 31 Times. The subtitle is ironic: 'When you're working with other people's words, there are clear rules of engagement.'"

SM: "I don't get the irony."

DB: "Apparently, what's good for the Op-Ed page is not good for the Sunday Magazine."

SM: "You need to clarify that for me."

DB: "Here is what the Op-Ed editor said his staff will do with submissions: 'Correct grammatical and typographical errors. Make sure that the article conforms to The New York Times Manual of Style and Usage. See to it that the article fits our allotted space. Fact-check the article.'"

SM: "Now I see where you are going with this."

DB: "Just for a moment, let's see what the Op-Ed editor says about fact-checking: 'While it is the author's responsibility to ensure that everything written for us is accurate, we still check facts - names, dates, places, quotations. We also check assertions. If news articles - from The Times or other publications - are at odds with a point or an example in an essay, we need to resolve whatever discrepancy exists.... we'd discuss it with the writer ... and we'd try to find a solution that preserves the writer's argument while also adhering to the facts.'"

SM: "So, if I understand the point you are making is that it was up to the Magazine editors to have the writer of that January 16 article verify the assertion about Dr. Hubbard having developed a profile similar to Dr. Dailey's."

DB: "Since Dr. Dailey's profile was a psychological one, all I asked for was the so-called 'evidence' that Dr. Hubbard created a psychological profile. The May 8 correction cleverly avoided that."

SM: "Okay. Let's go on to Dr. Hubbard's book."

CHAPTER TWENTY NINE —
THE HUBBARD HUBBUB

DB: "Dr. Hubbard undertook a psychiatric look at hijacking in his 1971 book. The inside cover is quite revealing: 'Virtually all of those interviewed proved to be effeminate, sexually inadequate, ineffectual, generally apolitical individuals who have skyjacked in situations of total personal failure as a decisive act to get themselves killed or at least out of this world. The offenders themselves tended to be sexually confused, weak moma's boys.' Dr. Hubbard also contended that hijackers were influenced by the force of gravity."

SM: "I must admit this seems to support your argument that he looked at skyjackers strictly from a psychiatric point of view."

DB: "He had some other interesting observations. On Pages 230 and 231, he proposed an international agreement for *'the immediate return of all offenders for hospitalization, study and disposition.'* He concluded that this agreement 'would put a stop to the crime in short order.' He also stressed research on the relationship between skyjackers and 'sexual inadequacy.'"

SM: "He certainly seems fixated on the sexuality of skyjackers."

DB: "I found a web site that noted Dr. Hubbard testified for the defense in a case involving a skyjacker identified only as 'Greg Ross.' Dr. Hubbard asserted that the defendant 'was schizophrenic, that he deserved to be treated not as a criminal but as a sick man and that hijackers often suffer from a sense of masculine failure and latent homosexuality.' Having said all of that, there is nothing in his book that shows how his psychiatric conclusions could be translated into a psychological screening of passengers."

SM: "By the way, what do you think of the Transportation Security Administration?"

CHAPTER THIRTY —
TSK, TSK, TSA

DB: "Having had my say, in the final analysis, I almost feel sorry for the TSA."

SM: "What do you mean by that?"

DB: "First, it had to absorb the FAA's Office of Civil Aviation Security, with its benign attitude about Mideast terrorists and potential hijacking of U.S. aircraft although we warned about that possibility as far back as 1978. Second, it had to try to implement sometimes conflicting procedures to screen passengers. As if those CAPPS systems weren't enough-of a headache, they were preceded by TIPs - Threat Image Protection-to check baggage for weapons. And, I don't even want to get into those Color Card warnings. But, in June 2005, The Washington Post reported, 'A new air-security system designed to track foreign visitors arriving in the United States has mistakenly snagged dozens of crew members of foreign airlines, according to new documents obtained from the Department of Homeland Security.' And, DHS is the boss of TSA. Having worked in government for nearly a quarter of a century, I know that political appointees dictate the programs that civil servants are forced to implement without question. Homeland Security Secretary Michael Chertoff had to face the wrath of members of a House Appropriations Subcommittee in March 2005 to defend the agency's budget. One subcommittee member called the agency 'dysfunctional.' Barely a month later, The Washington Post reported that TSA chief David

M. Stone was resigning, citing 'budget constraints and changes in leadership.' The ranking Democrat on the agency's oversight committee, Congressman Peter A. DeFazio of California, was cited as fearing 'Stone's departure signals a push by Republicans to dismantle the TSA and replace federal airport screeners, with ones employed by private companies.'"

SM: "Doesn't sound promising."

DB: "As if that were not enough, The Post followed up that story with one noting that 'Stone is the third top administrator to leave the three-year-old agency. The TSA has been plagued by operational missteps, public relations blunders and criticism of its performance from the public and legislators.' It gets even better. 'Its (No Fly) list has mistakenly snared senators. Its security screeners have been arrested for stealing from luggage, and its passenger pat-downs have set off an outcry from women.'"

SM: "And, you feel sorry for both DHS and TSA?"

DB: "I feel sorry for those who want to do a good job, but are like the proverbial lemmings marching down to the sea behind the Pied Piper of Hamelin. They just don't have a choice because chief decision makers are trying to address a criminal problem with a political solution."

SM: "Well, on that note, I want to thank you for sharing your thoughts with me, and for being so candid. Good luck on your book."

DB: "And, good luck on the hearings."

CHAPTER THIRTY ONE —
FINAL THOUGHTS

There will be those who read this far and say, "Been there, done that," regarding airline screening and its relationship to terrorism in general.

The point of this book is to plead for a sound process in creating the most effective, efficient, and least intrusive screening system. Too many cooks are stirring the bureaucratic cauldron of terrorism, each one determining the right taste.

I reiterate that our Task Force was successful because it "thought outside the bureaucratic box." Our group played devil's advocate with one another every step of the way. We tried to anticipate what effect our procedure would have on potential hijackers, the public, and the media. We were staunchly apolitical.

What seems to be escaping those with whom I have discussed this book is the fact that our work enabled us to predict, literally and figuratively, what was to happen on 9/11. It was just a logical extension of our work. We also readily agreed that no one effort would stem the tide of hijacking, only deter it to a manageable number. What law enforcement official will assert that crime can be eliminated?

Terrorist airplane hijackings have been around for a long time. The twain does meet.

We took great pains to look at every possibility, even among the some 200 ideas submitted to us, no matter how ludicrous they seemed to be. We did not want to be accused of bureaucratically dismissing or overlooking anything using the excuse, "That's not the way it's been done before."

As to The New York Times, I remain professionally offended on two counts. One, the paper has stained the singular accomplishment of my friend and colleague, Dr. John T. Dailey. Two, The Times remains guilty of sloppy and hypocritical journalism.

EPILOGUE

Not one word of what was said here ever appeared in the 9/11 Commission's Final Report.

Neither of my two unique books on airline passenger screening and Mideast terrorism ever will make it to The New York Times Best Seller List.

The Times never revealed its Sunday Magazine article's "anonymous source" to justify its continuing assertion that a **psychiatrist** created a second **psychological** study like the one developed by Dr. John T. Dailey. In an August 28, 2005 Public Editor column in The Times, the aforementioned Mr. Siegel was quoted as saying that "if it isn't obvious from the story why we permitted the material to be used anonymously, what was the rationale? What were the attempts to go back to the source?" The Times may be guilty of hypocrisy in my case.

On August 13, 2005, The Washington Post reported on Page 1 that Edmund S. Hawley, administrator of the Transportation Security Administration, "directed his staff to propose changes in how the agency screens 2 million passengers a day." Not only will the ban on various carry-on items be lifted, but "passengers no longer (will) routinely be required to remove their shoes at security checkpoint," the article noted. The headline read: "Airline Security Changes Planned." The sub-headline was: "Threats Reassessed to Make Travel Easier for Public." Read my tips, Administrator Hawley.

On August 30, 2005, the "On the Road" column in The New York Times quoted former Secretary of Homeland Security Tom Ridge as admitting, "I have been pulled into secondary inspection about a dozen times since I became a private citizen." It also cited Ridge as saying, "We need to move from looking for weapons to paying attention to people who are or could be terrorists."

ABOUT THE AUTHOR

David H. Brown began a 24-year federal career in 1967 as assistant director of information at the Department of Justice. He later transferred to the Federal Aviation Administration, then to the Department of Transportation, and in 1974 became the first professional public affairs officer at the Government Printing Office, retiring in 1991. In 1976, Mr. Brown founded and was first president of the National Association of Government Communicators. So, he understands government.

An Infantry rifleman in World-War II, the author later began a 28-year career as an Army Reserve officer, retiring as a lieutenant colonel in 1978. For the final 12 years, he had a mobilization assignment with the Office of the Chief of Information in the Pentagon. Mr. Brown also graduated from the 4-year 2-week Advanced Infantry Course at Fort Benning, Georgia, where tactics were discussed at length. In addition, he attended a two-week seminar on Cold War Strategy at the Army Command and General Staff College at Fort Leavenworth, Kansas. Further, in 1959, he was part of a 15-member Joint Information Task Force to deal with reporters from all over the U.S. who covered the first post-World War II exercise to determine how successfully thousands of troops could be airlifted to Ramey Air Force Base in Puerto Rico, called Operation Big Slam/Puerto Pine. Mr. Brown's World War II military decorations include the

Meritorious Service Medal, Combat Infantry Badge, and Bronze Star Ribbon with battle star. So, he understands the military.

Starting as a copy boy at The Cleveland Press, Mr. Brown later worked at the Circleville Herald, became state editor of The Columbus Citizen, and returned to The Press, spanning nearly 15 years on Ohio newspapers. He developed and taught media relations courses at the Department of Agriculture Graduate School, and taught journalism courses at a community college. During two newspaper strikes, the author worked at two local television stations. So, he understands the media

In 1967, he was the sole government spokesman at the Lorton, Virginia detention facility where the 600 Pentagon demonstrators were held for three days. During 1969-70, the author was the spokesman for the Federal Aviation Administration's Task Force on Deterrence of Air Piracy that developed the original airline passenger screening system. In 1971, he was the government spokesman at Fort Dix, New Jersey at the press conference announcing training of armed sky marshals. So, he understands government, the military, and the news media.

Mr. Brown believes there is a connection between present day *Mideast terrorist* hijacking of U.S. aircraft and the *non-terrorist* hijacking of U.S. aircraft more than three decades ago:

> "First, if you want to deal with hijackers, you have to think like hijackers. We accomplished that when Task Force member and then FAA chief psychologist Dr. John T. Dailey developed a list of some two dozen characteristics common to most hijackers into a behavioral profile that would help identify potential hijackers. I was on the team that tested the profile at nine airports, discovering that it fit no more than 2 percent of the flying public screened. We concluded such a small number of "suspects" would enable the system to

quickly clear the other 98 percent. And, that should still be the basis for current screening procedures - quickly clear the innocent.

"Second, if you want to deal with terrorists, you have to understand terrorism. In essence, terrorists are guerilla fighters. They are not necessarily clearly organized as our troops are. They seek political or even religious objectives, while we are concerned with military objectives. I fear that time is more on the side of Mideast terrorists than on ours.

"Third, efforts to deal with terrorism must be flexible. This is evidenced in the variety of locations and types of tactics the terrorists use. Dr. Dailey always maintained that his profile of 1969-70 fit only those times.

"The Task Force Final Report in 1978, which is FAA Manual AM-78-35, contained enough warnings about the possibility that terrorists might hijack U.S. aircraft so that 9/11 could have been prevented. Intelligence dysfunctions notwithstanding, all that our decision makers had to do was connect the dots between our predictions and terrorist activity such as the 1993 World Trade Center bombing that was highly publicized in the media."

www.ingramcontent.com/pod-product-compliance
Lightning Source LLC
Chambersburg PA
CBHW032059280526
45784CB00012B/134